Addressing the
UNPRODUCTIVE
CLASSROOM BEHAVIOURS of
STUDENTS WITH SPECIAL NEEDS

First published in 2010
by Jessica Kingsley Publishers
116 Pentonville Road
London N1 9JB, UK
and
400 Market Street, Suite 400
Philadelphia, PA 19106, USA

www.jkp.com

Copyright © Steve Chinn 2010
Printed digitally since 2011

Library of Congress Cataloging in Publication Data
Chinn, Stephen J.
  Addressing the unproductive classroom behaviours of students with special needs / Steve Chinn.
      p. cm.
  Includes index.
  ISBN 978-1-84905-050-0 (alk. paper)
  1. Learning disabled children--Education. 2. Behavior disorders in children. I. Title.

  LC4818.5.C47 2010
  371.9'04--dc22

                                        2009028524

British Library Cataloguing in Publication Data
A CIP catalogue record for this book is available from the British Library

ISBN 978 1 84905 050 0

This book is dedicated to the 'Comenius Team' –

ANGELA, HANS, JULIE, ROB AND THERESE

All the author's royalties from this book will be donated to the Majika Project, South Africa. The Majika School is an inspiring school, located in a township near the Kruger Park. The Majika Project is backed by the Anglican Diocese of Mpumalanga.

Contents

Introduction

This is not a book about bad behaviour, it is a book about the unproductive *classroom behaviours* exhibited (but not exclusively) by children or students with one of six learning disabilities – dyslexia, dyspraxia, attention deficit disorder/attention deficit hyperactivity disorder (ADD/ADHD), Asperger syndrome/autistic spectrum disorder, physical disabilities and speech and language disorders – and suggestions on how to address those behaviours. An example of the behaviours addressed is 'unable to work on group tasks'.

The recommendations in this book for classroom management of these behaviours are mostly at early levels of intervention. The rationale behind the first part of this book is to manage the classroom behaviours before they become one of the causes that may take the pupil towards unacceptable bad behaviour patterns.

> Ask teachers what they fear most about bad behaviour and they'll probably say fights, knives and chairs through windows. But ask them what the most common bad behaviour they experience is and they'll talk about calling out, not bringing pencils, chatting at inappropriate times – or low-level disruption. … Low-level disruption is like kryptonite for the well-planned lesson. (Bennett 2009, p.12)

The book looks at the management of the behaviours in three stages:

- Identification and monitoring.
- 'What to do on Monday' strategies.
- An overview of some of the theories that explain the underlying factors that may have contributed to the formation of the behaviours and can provide the skills to deal with behaviours beyond the 'What to do on Monday' level.

It is hoped that the overview of some influential concepts in the second part of this book will provide a deeper understanding that will enable teachers and support assistants to develop and adapt their own interventions to the needs of a particular pupil. Sometimes 'What to do on Monday' doesn't deal with the rest of the week. The content in this part of the book is to help develop understanding, empathy and flexibility of responses – to develop the skills to understand and control.

It is important to remember that not all children with learning difficulties exhibit maladaptive behaviour patterns. Apart from this being a rational statement, it is also a conclusion from a longitudinal study carried out in the USA (McKinney 1990).

WHAT THIS BOOK OFFERS

- A screener for pupils with special needs based on classroom observations.
- Checklists to help in identifying the classroom behaviours of pupils with a particular special need.
- How to set up practical and realistic individual behaviour plans.
- An overview of critical factors which underpin behaviours: communication skills, social skills and attributional style.
- Ways of addressing low-level classroom behaviours (before they develop into more serious concerns).
- A discussion of some of the factors that may contribute to a positive classroom ethos for pupils with special needs.

THE BACKGROUND TO THIS BOOK

This book is one outcome of the cooperative work of six European teachers – Hans Harmsen, Julie Kay, Therese McPhillips, Angela Power, Rob van Elswijk and Steve Chinn.

Inclusion is an accepted principle for schools worldwide. Consequently, teachers have to manage the behaviours of children with special needs who are now included in their classroom. This book is written for those teachers and for learning support assistants.

PART 1

CLASSROOM BEHAVIOURS

CHAPTER 1

CLASSROOM BEHAVIOURS and the AFFECTIVE DOMAIN

This book is not about how to teach maths, chemistry, history or any other subject to pupils with special needs. It is about helping this group of potentially vulnerable pupils to function more effectively in all subjects in all mainstream classrooms. Classroom behaviours are influenced by cognitive and emotional or affective abilities.

Obviously the content and structure of any academic curriculum is vital to the education of our children, but there is increasing awareness of the need to address non-cognitive issues too, for example, this list, advising what we, as teachers, should consider, is from a recent UK policy document (Department for Education and Skills 2001):

Approaches to learning
Learning style
Ability to concentrate
The influence of low reading skills, spelling skills, writing skills and maths skills on attention span and motivation

Communication
Receptive skills
Expressive skills
Social use of language
Ability to use subject language
Non-verbal communication skills
Use of signing

Social and emotional
Relationship with peers
Relationship with adults
Play skills
Social skills
Behaviour and its impact on others
Self-esteem and self-confidence

Level of independence
Ability to respond in an appropriate manner

Physical, sensory and medical
Gross and fine motor skills
Vision
Hearing
Medical conditions
Access needs

As can be seen from these headings, the need for teachers and learning support assistants (LSAs) to be able to comment on and evaluate progress in non-cognitive domains is necessary for all special needs pupils. Although it is close to stating the obvious, it is helpful to remember that we are teaching the whole child and that each child is very much an individual with different levels of abilities and deficits in each of the above areas and even then, those abilities and deficits vary from day to day and even within a day.

There will be strong influences and interactions between behaviours and curriculum, for example:

A seven-year-old, whose class were asked to hold up number fan cards for the number 'after' nine, held up ten. When the teacher switched to the number 'before' nine, the child held up his ten card again, looked around and saw that everyone else had held up eight. At that point he started to use his number fan as a pretend gun, and disrupt the lesson. It took so little to switch him off maths and turn him into a behaviour problem. (Jean Gross, TES letters, 19 December 2008)

In 1960s communist Russia, psychologists did not believe in the normal distribution for intelligence. All children had the same potential. It could be claimed that our curriculum is controlled by the normal distribution, in the sense that curriculum design focuses on the hump in the middle and ignores the tails at each end. The special needs children at the low end of the distribution often get their curriculum as an afterthought.

CHAPTER 2

The CHARACTERISTICS of the SPECIAL NEEDS IDENTIFIED as MOST PREVALENT

Our survey of over 220 teachers in three European countries identified the six special needs that were most prevalent in inclusive classrooms:

- attention deficit disorder/attention deficit hyperactivity disorder (ADD/ADHD)
- autistic spectrum/Asperger syndrome
- dyslexia
- dyspraxia
- speech and language disorder
- physical disability.

Although the survey did not provide sufficient information on the existence of 'rare disorders' (because they are rare) and other less frequently occurring disorders such as Tourette syndrome in classrooms, Chapter 5 will discuss some of the issues around these special needs.

We live in an ever-changing and evolving educational world. When I began teaching in 1967 the very caring school where I began my career helped an Advanced level physics student who wrote words spelled phonetically, in a broad Somerset accent. We were not aware of dyslexia. Later I worked with a boy whose parents, some years after he had left, criticized me for not recognizing that he had Asperger syndrome. When he left the school, in 1981, we in the UK did not know of the syndrome.

THE CHARACTERISTICS OF THE SIX SPECIAL NEEDS HIGHLIGHTED BY THE SURVEY

Having identified the most frequently encountered special needs from our survey, we then focused on researching the key characteristics for each special need. Our sources included the societies and associations that represent each special need, key texts and the collective experiences and knowledge of our research group. Of course, it is the individual nature of children that all of the characteristics for a specific special need are unlikely to be present for every child. A child cannot and should not be defined and described by a label alone. Also, to stress even further the individual nature of pupils with special needs, it is important to be aware that the level of severity of the manifestations of each characteristic will be different with each pupil and may even differ from day to day or even within a day for an individual student.

It is worth noting that any of these specific characteristics can and will also occur in students who will never warrant a diagnosis of special needs. Recently some educators have suggested that special needs are a variation of the 'normal' rather than a specific medical condition. Whatever the beliefs about special needs, it is manifestly obvious that the behaviours identified by our survey are not unique to the special needs population.

ATTENTION DEFICIT DISORDER / ATTENTION DEFICIT HYPERACTIVITY DISORDER (ADD/ADHD)

ADD/ADHD is a neuro-biological disorder that affects the ability to concentrate and remain focused on a task. People with ADHD usually have symptoms that define them as having one of three subtypes of the condition. The subtypes are:

- ADHD manifesting as mainly inattentive behaviour
- ADHD manifesting as mainly hyperactive-impulsive
- ADHD combined.

For example, if students have symptoms of all three behavioural problems – inattentiveness, hyperactivity and impulsiveness – they may have ADHD combined, which is the most common subtype of ADHD. Alternatively, if students have symptoms of inattentiveness, but not hyperactivity, or impulsiveness, they may have ADHD manifesting as mainly inattentive. This form of ADHD is also known as attention deficit disorder (ADD).

Childhood ADHD is more commonly diagnosed in boys than in girls, but this may be due to a tendency for the diagnosis to look for disruptive behaviour, which is more noticeable and tends to be more common in boys than girls. Girls with ADHD often have the mainly inattentive form of the condition, which may make them quiet and dreamy, and this can sometimes go unnoticed. As a result, some research suggests that ADHD could be under-diagnosed in girls, and could be more common than previously thought (see ADD Journeys 2009).

A pupil with ADHD may display some of the following characteristics. The pupil may

- have difficulty sustaining attention on tasks
- appear not to listen to what is being said to them
- not follow through with instructions
- have difficulty organizing tasks
- often lose things necessary for a task
- be easily distracted by irrelevant stimuli
- be forgetful in activities, forgetting to bring the necessary equipment (pens, books, etc.)
- blurt out answers to questions before the questions have been completed
- be frequently out of his or her seat at inappropriate times
- have difficulty waiting for his or her turn in games or group situations
- fidget with hands or feet
- run or climb about in inappropriate situations
- be impulsive, for example, always calling out in class and wanting to speak now
- not be a team player whether in the classroom or in games
- not do what the class is supposed to be doing
- be aggressive to classmates
- bother classmates, stopping them from concentrating
- daydream and be oblivious to the world around them.

Now we shall look at some of the characteristics of ADHD in more detail.

Inattentiveness

The student may

- have a very short attention span
- be very easily distracted
- be unable to stick at tasks that are perceived as tedious, or time consuming
- be unable to listen to, or carry out, instructions
- be unable to concentrate
- constantly change activity, or task.

Hyperactivity

The student may

- be unable to sit still, especially in calm or quiet surroundings
- constantly fidget
- be unable to settle to tasks
- display excessive physical movement.

Impulsiveness

The student may

- be unable to wait for a turn
- act without thinking
- break rules
- have little or no sense of danger.

If pupils have ADHD, their symptoms usually become noticeable at around the age of five. ADHD can cause many problems in the child's life, and can often lead to underachievement at school, poor social interaction with other children and adults, and problems with discipline. The characteristics of these pupils as described above go some way towards explaining why they are at risk in school situations, for example, being unable to sit still when the rest of the class is quiet, and being unable to wait for a turn.

Although it is not always the case, a student may also have other problems or conditions alongside ADHD. Some examples are given below.

Anxiety disorder

Some children with ADHD may have an anxiety disorder which causes them to worry and to be nervous much of the time. They may also have physical symptoms, such as a rapid heartbeat, sweating and dizziness.

Oppositional defiant disorder (ODD)

Oppositional defiant disorder (ODD) is manifested by negative and disruptive behaviour, particularly towards authority figures, such as parents and teachers. It is common among children with ADHD.

Conduct disorder

Children who have conduct disorder have a tendency towards highly antisocial behaviour, such as stealing, fighting, vandalism, and harming people and animals. This is a serious situation and will require professional help as soon as possible.

Sleep problems

Children with ADHD, who are very hyperactive, may find it difficult to settle to sleep at night, and may experience irregular sleeping patterns.

Tourette syndrome

Tourette syndrome is a condition of the central nervous system that causes involuntary movements and sounds (see also Chapter 5).

Learning difficulties

It is thought that up to 35 per cent of children with ADHD also have learning difficulties. However, it is important to remember that ADHD itself has no effect on intelligence.

Some manifestations of attention deficit disorder may be a consequence of other difficulties. For example, a pupil who has difficulties with computation may have a limited attention span in arithmetic lessons.

One of the conclusions drawn in a longitudinal study by McKinney (1990) was that children in both his attention deficit and problem behaviour subtypes had low task orientation and low academic productivity. 'The presence of these behaviours by themselves may be sufficient to establish risk for poorer academic progress early in the elementary period, which is then exacerbated by the social/emotional sequelae that develop subsequently'. (McKinney 1990, p.135).

McKinney reiterated his opinions on the benefits of early intervention in the closing paragraph of his chapter in Torgesen (1990).

AUTISTIC SPECTRUM / ASPERGER SYNDROME

Autism is a complex developmental disability that affects social and communication skills and impairs thought and imagination. (The number of children aged 6 to 21 with autism in US schools rose steadily from 5415 in 1991–1992 to 118,602 in 2001–2002 (Yazbak 2003).)

A pupil with this special need may

- have difficulty with social relationships, for example, appearing indifferent to other people or making odd, naive social approaches

- have difficulty with verbal and non-verbal communication, for example, not interpreting and understanding facial expressions, gestures or tone of voice

- have limited imagination and thus may pursue an activity rigidly and repetitively
- be wary of strangers
- have very poor language skills ranging from no spoken language to using meaningless phrases repeatedly
- show intense preoccupation with specific objects or topics
- experience sensory sensitivity, that is be over- or under-sensitive to sound, sight, smell, touch and taste
- rock, spin, flap their hands to stimulate sensation, to help with posture or balance, or to deal with stress
- have difficulty making predictions, use their imagination, understand the concept of danger, cope with unfamiliar situations or adjust to new situations.

Asperger syndrome is used to describe people at the higher functioning end of the autistic spectrum. They have fewer problems with language than those with autism but a typical manifestation is that they can be over-literal.

A pupil with this special need may

- find it hard to understand body language, facial expressions, gestures and tone of voice
- carry on talking regardless of the listener's interest
- stand too close when in conversation
- find it hard to make friends
- find it hard to think in abstract ways
- develop an almost obsessive interest in a hobby, a topic or collection
- be inflexible about specific routines or rituals
- take things literally and be pedantic
- become uneasy if routines change or if asked to try something new
- appear insensitive to the feelings or views of the listener
- demonstrate abnormal non-verbal communication, such as problems with eye contact, facial expressions, body postures, or gestures
- have an inability to return social or emotional feelings.

Asperger syndrome was not identified in English schools until the early 1990s. It was there, of course, but it was not the subject of any research paper in English. Special needs is not a field that has been finally defined or classified as yet; for example, dyscalculia is not discussed in this book.

DYSLEXIA

Dyslexia is a specific learning difficulty that hinders the learning of literacy skills. The problem is neurologically based and tends to run in families. The definition currently used by the International Dyslexia Association of the USA is as follows:

> Dyslexia is a specific learning disability that is neurological in origin. It is characterized by difficulties with accurate and/or fluent word recognition and by poor spelling and decoding abilities. These difficulties typically result from a deficit in the phonological component of language that is often unexpected in relation to other cognitive abilities and the provision of effective classroom instruction. Secondary consequences may include problems in reading comprehension and reduced reading experience that can impede growth of vocabulary and background knowledge. (Reid Lyon, Shaywitz and Shaywitz 2003, p.2)

It is thought that some four per cent of the population have severe dyslexia with a further six per cent experiencing significant difficulties. A pupil with dyslexia may

- have difficulty with letter knowledge, in linking sounds with symbols and in blending letters
- have difficulties with reading, writing and spelling
- spell the same word several different ways in the same essay
- overlook small words such as 'not' when reading
- have difficulties learning things by heart
- be a slow processor of some information
- be disorganized in much of what she or he does
- have difficulties with sequencing (remembering information in the correct sequence or following sequential instructions)
- appear to be more able than their written work suggests
- have a weak short-term memory and working memory (in capacity and duration)
- get very tired at the end of a school day
- have relatives with similar difficulties
- have low self-esteem
- become uneasy if routines change or when asked to try something new.

The characteristics of any special need will interact with the situation and circumstances the child meets. As the circumstances change with age, the characteristics may also evolve. I have illustrated this for dyslexia.

Symptoms of dyslexia in young children

In some cases, it may be possible to detect symptoms of dyslexia before a child starts school.

Possible symptoms include:

- experiencing a delay, or difficulty, in developing clear speech
- mixing up certain words and phrases – for example, saying 'by mall' instead of 'my ball'
- being unusually clumsy and uncoordinated
- finding it difficult to appreciate rhymes, for example, they cannot understand the connection between the words 'hat' and 'cat'
- having persistent problems with dressing, or tying their shoelaces.

(Of course, children develop at different rates. Some of these characteristics may simply be a result of developmental lag.)

Symptoms of dyslexia in children aged between five and seven years

Common symptoms of dyslexia in children aged between five and seven include:

- finding it difficult to learn the alphabet
- being unable to read, except for a few simple words
- having problems writing clearly
- having difficulty telling left from right, particularly as instructions (e.g. turn left)
- being unable to remember simple sequences, such as the days of the week
- having a low attention span, and problems concentrating (more noticeable when involved in tasks that they find challenging).

Symptoms of dyslexia in children aged between seven and twelve years

Common symptoms of dyslexia in children aged between seven and twelve include:

- making poor progress at school compared to their classmates

- becoming frustrated at school, which can lead either to behavioural problems, or to withdrawal
- being unable to learn the 'harder' (3x, 6x, 7x, 8x, 9x) multiplication tables
- having problems following a sequence of instructions, or remembering more than one thing at a time.

Symptoms of dyslexia in teenagers

Common symptoms of dyslexia in teenagers include:

- having difficulty in organizing work and work schedules
- experiencing problems copying, or writing down work and general speed of working
- having difficulty revising for, and coping emotionally with exams
- taking much longer than 'average' pupils to do school work
- producing written work in sufficient or acceptable quantity
- continuing problems with spelling and writing
- experiencing severe difficulties in learning a foreign language (which may also interfere with tenuously held knowledge of spelling and reading in English).

Dyslexia is the most commonly occurring of the six difficulties or disabilities selected for the study. In theory, provision and support for students with dyslexia is now readily available from primary school to higher education and, largely speaking, no longer a controversial issue. Reality may differ from theory in some regions.

DYSPRAXIA

Dyspraxia is an impairment or immaturity of the organization of movement. In many individuals there may be associated problems with language, perception and thought. Dyspraxia is not well understood and some experts in the field feel that it is not well defined at present. One of the main UK organizations for people with dyspraxia describes it as 'neuro-diversity' rather than disability.

A pupil with this special need may

- have difficulty adapting to a structured school routine
- be clumsy and prone to accidents
- have difficulty using a knife and fork
- have difficulties with physical education

- be slow at dressing and have problems tying shoelaces (Velcro to the rescue!)

- have poor handwriting, drawing and copying skills

- have limited concentration and poor listening skills

- be unable to remember more than two or three instructions at one time

- be slow to complete class work and homework

- have problems with coordination

- be messy, disorganized and prone to working in cluttered personal environments

- have unclear speech and be unable to pronounce some words

- have uncontrolled pitch, volume and rate when speaking.

The child's eye movements may be less subject to control, resulting in problems with tracking, difficulties in following a moving object smoothly with eyes without excessive head movement and a tendency to lose their place while reading. Eye movement can also create problems with relocating, that is changing focus quickly and effectively from one object to another (for example, looking from a whiteboard to an exercise book).

Problems with visual and auditory perception may also include being over-sensitive to light and having a difficulty in distinguishing sounds from background noise and a tendency to be over-sensitive to noise. The child may be over-sensitive or under-sensitive to touch, which can result in dislike of being touched and/or an aversion to over-loose or tight clothing and a general tactile defensiveness. The child may be able to do only one thing at a time properly, though he or she still may try to do many things at once. The child may have difficulty forming relationships with others and become isolated in class, which may be partially due to poor social skills such as being tactless, interrupting frequently and problems with teamwork.

Gross motor and fine motor problems

The problems associated with dyspraxia may be due to gross motor and/or fine motor problems. Problems with gross motor coordination skills (large movements) may include the following:

- Poor balance, which results in problems such as difficulty in riding a bicycle, or walking up and down hills.

- Weak muscle tone can cause poor posture and fatigue, resulting in problems such as a difficulty in standing for a long time. Also there can be problems with floppy, unstable joints. Some people with dyspraxia may have flat feet.

- Poor hand–eye coordination can result in difficulty with sports, especially those which involve catching, hitting or kicking a ball.

- There may be lack of rhythm when dancing, or doing aerobics.

- Clumsy gait and movement can include a difficulty in changing direction.

- Exaggerated 'accessory movements' such as flapping arms can occur when running.

- A tendency to fall, trip or bump into things and people may be due to a lack of awareness of body position in space and spatial relationships.

Problems with fine motor coordination skills (small movements) accompanied by a lack of manual dexterity may include the following:

- Poor competence in two-handed tasks may cause problems with activities such as using cutlery, craft work and playing musical instruments.

- Poor manipulative skills can result in difficulties such as typing, handwriting and drawing and, as a consequence of a poor pen grip, pressing too hard when writing and difficulty when writing along a line.

- Difficulty with dressing and grooming activities, such as combing hair, fastening clothes and tying shoelaces, will make them the last to change for games.

- Being over-sensitive or under-sensitive to touch can result in a dislike of being touched and/or an aversion to over-loose or tight clothing and a general tactile defensiveness.

- The person may do only one thing at a time properly, although they may try to do several things at once.

- Being slow to finish tasks may be linked to a tendency to daydream and wander about aimlessly.

Note that many of the characteristics listed are, of course, not unique to people with dyspraxia. Not even the most severe cases of dyspraxia will have all the characteristics listed above.

Dyspraxia sometimes co-occurs with other specific learning differences such as ADHD, dyslexia and Asperger syndrome. The particular combination of dyspraxia and ADHD is sometimes referred to as DAMP (Disorders of Attention, Motor control and Perception).

SPEECH AND LANGUAGE DISORDER

There is a group of children who do not develop language skills normally irrespective of any obvious intellectual or physical disability. These children are said to have a specific or primary speech or language impairment, which may occur in isolation or alongside other disabilities.

Speech and language disorders refer to problems in communication and related areas such as oral motor function. These delays and disorders range from simple sound substitutions to the inability to understand or use language or use the oral-motor mechanism for functional speech. Some causes of speech and language disorders include hearing loss, neurological disorders, brain injury, mental retardation, drug abuse and physical impairments such as cleft palate and voice abuse.

Speech and language disorders are varied and can occur at any age. They affect a pupil's ability to interact and communicate and can interfere with the pupil's ability to understand, to express his or her thoughts, or to be understood. The causes of speech and language disorders are varied and may be present from birth, or they can occur in childhood or later in life due to accident or illness. Frequently the cause is not known.

Since the ability to communicate is essential in life and in school, these students are significantly handicapped. A pupil may have both a speech and a language disorder, or have one without the other.

A student with this special need may

- be late in learning how to speak
- have a discrepancy between verbal and non-verbal skills or between receptive and expressive language
- lack concentration and seem inattentive
- have problems with short-term memory
- have word-finding difficulties
- be unable to understand or express themselves clearly
- not understand jokes, puns or sarcasm
- take meanings literally
- have a tendency to agree rather than voice opposition
- stutter
- lack confidence and have a poor self-concept
- avoid social interaction including group activities
- exhibit class clown behaviour.

Expressive and receptive communication is vital to absorbing and succeeding in education, at whatever level that education takes place.

PHYSICAL DISABILITIES

Physical disabilities encompass a wide range of special needs, including cerebral palsy, loss of or damage to limbs, brittle bone disease, low muscle tone, muscular dystrophy, spina bifida, weak motor skills and so on.

All of the special needs pupils who have a physical difficulty may

- have difficulty with mobility
- take longer to complete a given task
- have coordination difficulties
- undergo emotional stress in dealing with their disability.

COMMON CHARACTERISTICS ACROSS THE SIX SPECIAL NEEDS (COMORBIDITY)

It is quite common for pupils to have a combination of two or more special needs, in part because the disabilities tend to have some characteristics in common, for example, poor short-term memory. The technical term for co-occurring difficulties is *comorbidity*. Co-occurrence may be due to shared and common factors within the two disorders. It may be a consequence, for example, ADD in arithmetic lessons may be a consequence of poor skills in computation.

The co-occurrence can also be completely unconnected. The disorders may be totally independent of each other. There are many characteristics in common between the six disabilities that feature in this book, particularly the first five listed, often making a diagnosis complicated. A full diagnosis should be, therefore, from a team of relevant experts.

However, in terms of managing these pupils in the mainstream classroom, the commonalities mean that if you address a particular characteristic of one pupil with a particular special need, it may well help other pupils with other special needs (and probably some students with lower levels of difficulty which may remain unrecognized and unidentified).

A label or labels help a teacher or learning support assistant, and thus the pupil, only if advice (and possibly resources) on how to address the needs is a consequence of having the label(s). Of course, it would be unproductive in so many ways to stereotype any student solely by his or her label.

Although this book is primarily concerned with classroom management issues, it does provide a starting point and an overview for understanding the need for appropriate social skills training and explains some of the emotional consequences of these special needs (which will influence and impact on classroom behaviours).

CHAPTER 3

The CLASSROOM BEHAVIOURS LIST (CBL)

The Classroom Behaviours List was compiled by six highly experienced special needs European teachers. It lists the 34 most frequently occurring behaviours that occurred in their own and in colleagues' classrooms.

The list was sent to over 200 teachers in schools in Ireland, the Netherlands and the UK; they were asked to grade each behaviour for each special needs pupil in their class, on a scale of one to five, defined as:

      1 = 'Never a problem'
      2 = 'Seldom a problem'
      3 = 'Occasionally a problem'
      4 = 'Frequently a problem'
      5 = 'Constantly a problem'

THE CLASSROOM BEHAVIOURS LIST (CBL)

Classroom behaviour	1	2	3	4	5
1. Slow to start work					
2. Refuses to do work					
3. Having the correct equipment					
4. Not starting work without individual instruction					
5. Completing written tasks					
6. Loses focus during tasks					
7. Accepting advice					
8. Accepting criticism from teacher					
9. Accepting criticism from peers					
10. Fiddles with pencils, multi-purpose tack … etc.					

Classroom behaviour	1	2	3	4	5
11. Distracts other students					
12. Interferes with other students' work					
13. Persists with bad behaviour despite correction					
14. Makes inappropriate comments in class					
15. Withdraws quietly from task					
16. Does not seek help even when needed					
17. Displays sudden verbal outbursts					
18. Displays sudden physical outbursts					
19. Displays sudden emotional outbursts					
20. Leaves seat for no reason					
21. Unable to work on group tasks					
22. Is not accepted by peer group in class					
23. Is not accepted by peer group outside classroom					
24. Misinterprets instructions					
25. Misinterprets social communication					
26. Blames others for own difficulties					
27. Blames themselves for difficulties					
28. Believes they will fail on a task before starting					
29. Sets unrealistic goals for themselves					
30. Thinks they cannot improve/learn					
31. Unable to form friendships					
32. Limited participation in social activities					
33. Seems unhappy in class					
34. Absence from school					

Most of the behaviours listed fall into three main categories. I shall keep returning to these categories throughout the book to explore different implications for both the teacher and the student:

- Classroom management and personal organization issues.
- Social skills and communication issues.
- Emotional support and guidance issues.

A particular behaviour may be placed in one group, but the underlying cause may have placed it in another group, for example, 'slow to start work' is placed in the Classroom Management group, but the reason the student is slow to start work could be caused by low self-esteem and low self-efficacy resulting in risk avoidance, which would place the behaviour in the Emotional Support group. A discussion with the pupil, at an appropriate time, should help to reveal any underlying causes.

Classroom management and personal organization issues

1. Slow to start work

3. Having the correct equipment

4. Not starting work without individual instruction

5. Completing written tasks

6. Loses focus during tasks

10. Fiddles with pencils, multi-purpose tack … etc.

20. Leaves seat for no reason

24. Misinterprets instructions

34. Absence from school

Social skills and communication issues

9. Accepting criticism from peers

11. Distracts other students

12. Interferes with other students' work

13. Persists with bad behaviour despite correction

14. Makes inappropriate comments in class

17. Displays sudden verbal outbursts

21. Unable to work on group tasks

22. Is not accepted by peer group in class

23. Is not accepted by peer group outside classroom

25. Misinterprets social communications

26. Blames others for own difficulties

31. Unable to form friendships

32. Limited participation in social activities

Emotional support and guidance issues

2. Refuses to do work

7. Accepting advice

8. Accepting criticism from teacher

15. Withdraws quietly from task

16. Does not seek help even when needed

19. Displays sudden emotional outbursts

27. Blames themselves for difficulties

28. Believes they will fail on a task before starting

29. Sets unrealistic goals for them selves

30. Thinks they cannot improve/learn

31. Seems unhappy in class

CHAPTER 4

The CBL PROFILES for EACH SPECIAL NEED

The Classroom Behaviours Lists below show the average rating given by teachers, for each behaviour for each of the six special needs groups.

Note: Pupils with ADD/ADHD and those on the autistic spectrum of difficulties generated higher average scores on most of the behaviours.

The collated results are shown on the six Classroom Behaviours Lists below. These lists and the main concerns for each special needs group can be photocopied and used as screeners in the classroom.

ADD/ADHD: CBL PROFILE

1 = 'Never a problem'; 2 = 'Seldom a problem'; 3 = 'Occasionally a problem';
4 = 'Frequently a problem'; 5 = 'Constantly a problem'

Classroom Behaviour	1	2	3	4	5
1. Slow to start work		X			
2. Refuses to do work			X		
3. Having the correct equipment			X		
4. Not starting work without individual instruction				X	
5. Completing written tasks					X
6. Loses focus during tasks					X
7. Accepting advice				X	
8. Accepting criticism from teacher				X	
9. Accepting criticism from peers					X
10. Fiddles with pencils, multi-purpose tack … etc.					X
11. Distracts other students					X
12. Interferes with other students' work					X
13. Persists with bad behaviour despite correction					X
14. Makes inappropriate comments in class				X	
15. Withdraws quietly from task				X	
16. Does not seek help even when needed				X	
17. Displays sudden verbal outbursts					X
18. Displays sudden physical outbursts				X	
19. Displays sudden emotional outbursts				X	
20. Leaves seat for no reason					X
21. Unable to work on group tasks					X
22. Is not accepted by peer group in class				X	
23. Is not accepted by peer group outside classroom				X	
24. Misinterprets instructions				X	
25. Misinterprets social communication					X
26. Blames others for own difficulties					X
27. Blames themselves for difficulties			X		
28. Believes they will fail on a task before starting				X	
29. Sets unrealistic goals for themselves			X		
30. Thinks they cannot improve/learn			X		
31. Unable to form friendships				X	
32. Limited participation in social activities				X	
33. Seems unhappy in class			X		
34. Absence from school		X			

✓

ADD/ADHD: main concerns from the CBL

- Completing written tasks
- Loses focus during tasks
- Accepting criticism from peers
- Fiddles with pencils, multi-purpose tack … etc.
- Distracts other students
- Interferes with other students' work
- Persists with bad behaviour despite correction
- Displays sudden verbal outbursts
- Leaves seat for no reason
- Unable to work on group tasks
- Misinterprets social communication
- Blames others for own difficulties

AUTISTIC SPECTRUM / ASPERGER SYNDROME CBL PROFILE

1 = 'Never a problem'; 2 = 'Seldom a problem'; 3 = 'Occasionally a problem';
4 = 'Frequently a problem' ; 5 = 'Constantly a problem'

Classroom Behaviour	1	2	3	4	5
1. Slow to start work					X
2. Refuses to do work			X		
3. Having the correct equipment			X		
4. Not starting work without individual instruction					X
5. Completing written tasks				X	
6. Loses focus during tasks					X
7. Accepting advice				X	
8. Accepting criticism from teacher					X
9. Accepting criticism from peers					X
10. Fiddles with pencils, multi-purpose tack … etc.					X
11. Distracts other students			X		
12. Interferes with other students' work			X		
13. Persists with bad behaviour despite correction			X		
14. Makes inappropriate comments in class			X		
15. Withdraws quietly from task					X
16. Does not seek help even when needed					X
17. Displays sudden verbal outbursts				X	
18. Displays sudden physical outbursts		X			
19. Displays sudden emotional outbursts				X	
20. Leaves seat for no reason			X		
21. Unable to work on group tasks					X
22. Is not accepted by peer group in class				X	
23. Is not accepted by peer group outside classroom				X	
24. Misinterprets instructions					X
25. Misinterprets social communication					X
26. Blames others for own difficulties			X		
27. Blames themselves for difficulties		X			
28. Believes they will fail on a task before starting				X	
29. Sets unrealistic goals for themselves		X			
30. Thinks they cannot improve/learn		X			
31. Unable to form friendships					X
32. Limited participation in social activities					X
33. Seems unhappy in class			X		
34. Absence from school	X				

✓

AUTISTIC SPECTRUM/ASPERGER SYNDROME: main concerns from the CBL

- Slow to start work
- Not starting work without individual instruction
- Loses focus during tasks
- Accepting criticism from teacher
- Accepting criticism from peers
- Fiddles with pencils, multi-purpose tack … etc.
- Withdraws quietly from task
- Does not seek help even when needed
- Unable to work on group tasks
- Misinterprets instructions
- Misinterprets social communication
- Unable to form friendships
- Limited participation in social activities

DYSLEXIA: CBL PROFILE

1 = 'Never a problem'; 2 = 'Seldom a problem'; 3 = 'Occasionally a problem';
4 = 'Frequently a problem'; 5 = 'Constantly a problem'

Classroom behaviour	1	2	3	4	5
1. Slow to start work					X
2. Refuses to do work		X			
3. Having the correct equipment				X	
4. Not starting work without individual instruction					X
5. Completing written tasks					X
6. Loses focus during tasks					X
7. Accepting advice			X		
8. Accepting criticism from teacher			X		
9. Accepting criticism from peers				X	
10. Fiddles with pencils, multi-purpose tack … etc.				X	
11. Distracts other students				X	
12. Interferes with other students' work			X		
13. Persists with bad behaviour despite correction			X		
14. Makes inappropriate comments in class			X		
15. Withdraws quietly from task				X	
16. Does not seek help even when needed				X	
17. Displays sudden verbal outbursts		X			
18. Displays sudden physical outbursts		X			
19. Displays sudden emotional outbursts		X			
20. Leaves seat for no reason			X		
21. Unable to work on group tasks			X		
22. Is not accepted by peer group in class	X				
23. Is not accepted by peer group outside classroom	X				
24. Misinterprets instructions					X
25. Misinterprets social communication			X		
26. Blames others for own difficulties			X		
27. Blames themselves for difficulties			X		
28. Believes they will fail on a task before starting				X	
29. Sets unrealistic goals for themselves			X		
30. Thinks they cannot improve/learn				X	
31. Unable to form friendships		X			
32. Limited participation in social activities		X			
33. Seems unhappy in class		X			
34. Absence from school		X			

Dyslexia: main concerns from the CBL

For the main concerns for dyslexic students I have included items rated as '4. frequent problem' as well as the items rated as '5. constant problem'. The inclusion of these items still keeps the list manageable.

- Slow to start work
- Having the correct equipment
- Not starting work without individual instruction
- Completing written tasks
- Loses focus during tasks
- Accepting criticism from peers
- Fiddles with pencils, multi-purpose tack … etc.
- Distracts other students
- Withdraws quietly from task
- Does not seek help even when needed
- Misinterprets instructions
- Believes they will fail on a task before starting
- Thinks they cannot improve/learn

DYSPRAXIA : CBL PROFILE

1 = 'Never a problem'; 2 = 'Seldom a problem'; 3 = 'Occasionally a problem';
4 = 'Frequently a problem'; 5 = 'Constantly a problem'

Classroom behaviour	1	2	3	4	5
1. Slow to start work					X
2. Refuses to do work		X			
3. Having the correct equipment			X		
4. Not starting work without individual instruction					X
5. Completing written tasks					X
6. Loses focus during tasks					X
7. Accepting advice			X		
8. Accepting criticism from teacher				X	
9. Accepting criticism from peers				X	
10. Fiddles with pencils, multi-purpose tack … etc.				X	
11. Distracts other students			X		
12. Interferes with other students' work				X	
13. Persists with bad behaviour despite correction		X			
14. Makes inappropriate comments in class		X			
15. Withdraws quietly from task		X			
16. Does not seek help even when needed				X	
17. Displays sudden verbal outbursts		X			
18. Displays sudden physical outbursts		X			
19. Displays sudden emotional outbursts		X			
20. Leaves seat for no reason		X			
21. Unable to work on group tasks				X	
22. Is not accepted by peer group in class			X		
23. Is not accepted by peer group outside classroom			X		
24. Misinterprets instructions					X
25. Misinterprets social communication				X	
26. Blames others for own difficulties		X			
27. Blames themselves for difficulties			X		
28. Believes they will fail on a task before starting				X	
29. Sets unrealistic goals for themselves			X		
30. Thinks they cannot improve/learn				X	
31. Unable to form friendships		X			
32. Limited participation in social activities			X		
33. Seems unhappy in class			X		
34. Absence from school	X				

✓

Dyspraxia: main concerns from the CBL

For the main concerns for dyspraxic students I have included items rated as '4. frequent problem' as well as the items rated as '5. constant problem'. The inclusion of these items still keeps the list manageable.

- Slow to start work
- Not starting work without individual instruction
- Completing written tasks
- Loses focus during tasks
- Fiddles with pencils, multi-purpose tack ... etc.
- Interferes with other students' work
- Does not seek help even when needed
- Unable to work on group tasks
- Believes they will fail on a task before starting
- Misinterprets instructions
- Thinks they cannot improve/learn

SPEECH AND LANGUAGE: CBL PROFILE

1 = 'Never a problem'; 2 = 'Seldom a problem'; 3 = 'Occasionally a problem';
4 = 'Frequently a problem'; 5 = 'Constantly a problem'

Classroom behaviour	1	2	3	4	5
1. Slow to start work			X		
2. Refuses to do work	X				
3. Having the correct equipment			X		
4. Not starting work without individual instruction				X	
5. Completing written tasks				X	
6. Loses focus during tasks					X
7. Accepting advice		X			
8. Accepting criticism from teacher	X				
9. Accepting criticism from peers			X		
10. Fiddles with pencils, multi-purpose tack … etc.					X
11. Distracts other students			X		
12. Interferes with other students' work		X			
13. Persists with bad behaviour despite correction		X			
14. Makes inappropriate comments in class		X			
15. Withdraws quietly from task				X	
16. Does not seek help even when needed				X	
17. Displays sudden verbal outbursts	X				
18. Displays sudden physical outbursts		X			
19. Displays sudden emotional outbursts		X			
20. Leaves seat for no reason			X		
21. Unable to work on group tasks			X		
22. Is not accepted by peer group in class	X				
23. Is not accepted by peer group outside classroom		X			
24. Misinterprets instructions					X
25. Misinterprets social communication				X	
26. Blames others for own difficulties		X			
27. Blames themselves for difficulties		X			
28. Believes they will fail on a task before starting			X		
29. Sets unrealistic goals for themselves		X			
30. Thinks they cannot improve/learn	X				
31. Unable to form friendships			X		
32. Limited participation in social activities			X		
33. Seems unhappy in class	X				
34. Absence from school		X			

✓

Speech and language: main concerns from the CBL

For the main concerns for students with speech and language disorders I have included six items rated as '4. frequent problem' as well as '5. constant problem'. The inclusion of these extra items still keeps the list manageable.

- Not starting work without individual instruction
- Completing written tasks
- Loses focus during tasks
- Fiddles with pencils, multi-purpose tack … etc.
- Withdraws quietly from task
- Does not seek help even when needed
- Misinterprets instructions
- Misinterprets social communication

PHYSICAL DISABILITIES: CBL PROFILE

1 = 'Never a problem'; 2 = 'Seldom a problem'; 3 = 'Occasionally a problem';
4 = 'Frequently a problem'; 5 = 'Constantly a problem'

Classroom behaviour	1	2	3	4	5
1. Slow to start work				X	
2. Refuses to do work	X				
3. Having the correct equipment	X				
4. Not starting work without individual instruction			X		
5. Completing written tasks				X	
6. Loses focus during tasks				X	
7. Accepting advice		X			
8. Accepting criticism from teacher	X				
9. Accepting criticism from peers	X				
10. Fiddles with pencils, multi-purpose tack … etc.			X		
11. Distracts other students		X			
12. Interferes with other students' work		X			
13. Persists with bad behaviour despite correction	X				
14. Makes inappropriate comments in class	X				
15. Withdraws quietly from task			X		
16. Does not seek help even when needed			X		
17. Displays sudden verbal outbursts	X				
18. Displays sudden physical outbursts	X				
19. Displays sudden emotional outbursts	X				
20. Leaves seat for no reason	X				
21. Unable to work on group tasks		X			
22. Is not accepted by peer group in class	X				
23. Is not accepted by peer group outside classroom	X				
24. Misinterprets instructions		X			
25. Misinterprets social communication		X			
26. Blames others for own difficulties	X				
27. Blames themselves for difficulties		X			
28. Believes they will fail on a task before starting			X		
29. Sets unrealistic goals for themselves		X			
30. Thinks they cannot improve/learn		X			
31. Unable to form friendships		X			
32. Limited participation in social activities			X		
33. Seems unhappy in class		X			
34. Absence from school		X			

✓

Physical disabilities: main concerns from the CBL

- Completing written tasks
- Loses focus during tasks
- Slow to start work

Note the low 'scores' for the behaviours for this group relative to the other five special needs.

CHAPTER 5

OTHER DISORDERS and RARE DISORDERS

The six special needs that are the focus of the first part of this book were selected on the basis of the frequency of their appearance in classrooms. Obviously, this method of selection excluded less frequently occurring disorders and rare disorders. This chapter addresses that omission for four reasons. The first is to draw attention to the fact that, even though rare, these students may well be included in mainstream classes. The second is to illustrate cases where behaviours are often the direct consequence of a medical condition. The third is to consider the impact of the disorder on behaviours that have a social skill component. The fourth is the interaction between the teaching methods used and the learning needs of the student. These all suggest that different approaches for intervention may be needed and that, once again, empathy and understanding remain fundamental to successful inclusion. In some respects with this group of students, teachers could be more vulnerable to accusations of discrimination or inappropriate reactions if the behaviour has an underlying and recognized medical cause.

Although this book is about students with special needs, any child can engage in a behaviour that is undesirable or inappropriate. Some 'inappropriate' behaviours are characteristic of developmental stages and are therefore 'appropriate' if viewed developmentally. If a student is developmentally delayed then the behaviour may be understandable and appropriate from a developmental perspective even if it is not acceptable from a chronological perspective. When a child or adolescent has been diagnosed as having a neurobehavioural condition, however, teachers may find themselves trying to determine whether the behaviour is voluntary or a symptom of the child's condition and then how to address it.

There are over 5000 known rare disorders. Over 200 are listed on the National Organization for Rare Disorders (NORD) website (www. rarediseases.org). An approximate rate of occurrence for a rare disorder is one in 2000.

In order to illustrate some important points I have selected three disorders for this chapter:

- Down syndrome
- Tourette syndrome
- Prader-Willi syndrome

The occurrence of Prader-Willi syndrome is between 1:15,000 and 1:25,000 (1:20,000) which means that about 2000–4000 people in the UK have this disorder. For Down syndrome the frequency is 1:720 and for the most severe form of Tourette syndrome the frequency is estimated to be 1:2000. These figures could be considered in terms of a large academy of 2000 students. Statistically, without considering the way inclusion is applied, this means there could be three students with Down syndrome per academy, one with Tourette syndrome per academy and one Prader-Willi syndrome student per ten academies.

One of the implications of these rates of occurrence is that teachers are unlikely to have enough experience to develop the knowledge required to deal with rare disorders. If the individuality of the manifestations of any disorder are added in then the chances of a teacher knowing what to do with a student with a rare disorder are poor. This could be an issue in policies such as 'Inclusion for All'. It also draws attention again to the need to provide awareness training for all staff should any of these disorders be present in a school. Consistency is a crucial requirement for successful inclusion of these vulnerable students. Training may help provide that consistency, but training may not have the same impact and outcome on all teachers. Training the other students in the school could also improve the school lives of pupils with these and similar disorders. Most interactions will come from other students, not from teachers.

DOWN SYNDROME

Reflecting a point made throughout this book, the UPS of Downs organization notes that 'There are no behaviour problems unique to children with Down syndrome' (UPS of Downs 2009). This statement will be true for all difficulties and disabilities. The problems may not be unique, but the approaches to intervention may well have to be carefully tailored to an individual student's needs.

Down syndrome is well known and recognized. Most Down syndrome children are recognizable with the consequence that others' expectations may adapt almost automatically. It seems likely that any of the behaviours they exhibit are the consequence of a developmental lag and the underlying traits such as a short concentration span and poor short-term memory. As is explained in Chapter 12, social skills and social competence require cognitive abilities that students with lower IQs may not have.

Classroom interaction between teacher and student may be helped if the teacher is aware that students with Down syndrome tend to be strong visual learners with poor auditory memory. If a teacher relies on too much talk, the student may struggle and a short attention span may become even shorter with the consequent risk of poor behaviour.

TOURETTE SYNDROME

Tourette syndrome is characterized by repetitive involuntary movements and vocalizations known as tics. Tics may be either simple or complex. Commonly occurring simple tics include eye blinking, head jerking, facial grimaces, grunting sounds or sniffing. Complex tics include distinct patterns of movement, hopping, bending, barking, words and phrases (coprolalia is the technical term for uttering swear words). Tics are often exacerbated by stress or excitement and reduced by calm and focused activities. The relevance of this information is that the tics are not controllable, they make the student vulnerable to bullying and poor social integration and that the calmer the classroom, the less likely they are to occur.

What is also interesting and relevant about these tics is that they are usually judged as undesirable behaviours if they are seen in a classroom. It could almost be an example of the classic attribution of 'It's not my fault.' The involuntary nature of these characteristics illustrates the need to be empathetic and appropriate in responding to behaviours. The principle of discussing issues with a student is highly pertinent here. Tourette syndrome frequently co-occurs with ADHD.

PRADER-WILLI SYNDROME

Prader-Willi syndrome is very rare. Teachers are unlikely to have met a student with this syndrome, which may well mean that they are unprepared to deal with the associated behaviours. Several of the characteristics typically associated with the syndrome are not conducive to acceptable classroom behaviours. Students may well have a low IQ, which will make the learning of social skills and competence difficult. This is exacerbated by an inclination to be stubborn, an inability to adapt to changes in routine (which can result in tantrums), adrenalin rushes and a tendency to become tired and sleepy. These particular characteristics illustrate the need to pick the moment for an intervention. An ill-timed intervention, however well meaning and seemingly appropriate for other students, could well turn a minor problem into a major problem.

CHAPTER 6

ELIMINATE the OBVIOUS

A teacher working with young offenders met a new student. In her initial appraisal of his educational needs, she quickly found that he was effectively a non-reader. When she checked his vision she found that he couldn't see the print on a page. He was 17 years old and no one had noticed this deficit. Once this problem had been addressed, she was able to teach him to read, a skill he mastered quite quickly.

Any behaviour can be affected by physical factors such as poor vision or poor hearing. It is often impossible for students to be aware of their difference, since they have never experienced an alternative against which they can make a judgement. It makes sense to screen for some of the factors that may affect the ability to receive information before initiating a complex behaviour programme.

VISION

Myopia (short-sightedness) will prevent students from seeing clearly what they are trying to read from a board or a book. It may also create fatigue so that reading quickly leads to tiredness and demotivation. Problems with being long sighted may handicap working from a book.

There are also more subtle problems with vision, such as Irlen syndrome. Some people find the contrast between white paper and black print makes the print blur or move. This is known as Irlen syndrome or scotopic sensitivity. The problem can be addressed by using colour filters (see Crossbow Education 2009) or coloured paper. Many websites for learning disabilities, especially dyslexia, have the facility to change the background colour and the colour of the font on the screen.

Some vision problems, such as field of vision, may need intervention from a behavioural optometrist (see British Association of Behavioural Optometrists (BABO) 2009).

HEARING

A student may have a weak general ability to receive sounds. Some people hear reasonably well, but are unable to hear some frequencies. The UK government has a controversial scheme which uses high frequency noise to make young people move away from trouble spots. Older people can no longer hear the high frequencies.

As an example of a subtle hearing loss, I taught a 13-year-old student who did not understand decimal numbers. As we discussed this problem it became apparent that he had never heard the end sound of the decimal word and, for example, could not hear the difference between 'hundred' and 'hundredth'. This was a major block to learning. Decimals were a mystery and his attention span in that topic area was minimal. Hearing can be about the frequencies you can and cannot hear. (National Deaf Children's Society 2009)

SHORT-TERM MEMORY

Poor short-term memory (STM) is often a feature of special needs. For example, I have taught many 13-year-old dyslexic students who had short-term memories restricted to three items (and occasionally fewer). This is an invisible but widely influential problem. The usual way it is revealed is in a failure, though it does not always follow in schools that the failure is attributed to STM deficits. Sometimes the pupil is accused of being inattentive. The following is a report from the support teacher for a 13-year-old girl who is having problems with maths:

I am constantly having to prompt Ellie to look at Mrs Smith and listen to her. She seems to spend a lot of time rubbing out and sharpening her pencil!

Mrs Smith paces the lessons very well and Ellie should be able to follow what she is teaching.

I also feel that Ellie has become rather lazy from the point of view of always saying she doesn't remember how to do any maths processes. She will seem to have grasped a concept yet the following lesson she will have forgotten it.

I am beginning to insist that she tries to remember how to do the work.

The reality is that Ellie cannot keep up with the 'well-paced' lessons and tries to make notes to help her remember what Mrs Smith says. Ellie has a poor short-term memory. As for 'I am beginning to insist that she tries to remember how to do the work', there is little or no empathy or awareness on display there! Sometimes the observations from the adult say more about the adult than they do about the student.

Generally secondary age students and adults will have STM for about six items and most people subconsciously work to that experience when communicating and giving out information. The reality for many students with special needs is a STM for maybe only two or three items.

Short-term memory is highly influential in many learning situations. For example, a teacher may give out a series of instructions at the start of a lesson. If the number of items in the list exceeds the STM of a pupil, then that pupil may forget all of the items and not be able to start the work (see CBL items 1, 2 and 6). This may be misinterpreted as a negative behaviour.

STM is also a factor in everyday life. I recently gave my credit card number over the phone. I gave it in four digit chunks. To my surprise, the operative said, 'Thank you, I wish all callers would do that and not say all 16 digits in one go.'

It is relatively easy to do a quick check on a student's STM. The check is normally done as digit span tests. The tester says two, three, four, five or six numerals, spaced at one-second intervals, and the student has to repeat them back. For example, the tester says, 'Eight, three, nine, one.' And the subject repeats them back, 'Eight, three, nine, one.'

Teachers should adjust the way they give instructions accordingly. STM is a fundamental and pervasive factor in communication for all students, but, once again, students with special needs are particularly vulnerable.

WORKING MEMORY

Working memory can be viewed as the next step up from short-term memory. Basically it is about manipulating information held in short-term memory. A good working memory is vital to being able to do mental arithmetic. Although mental arithmetic is often seen as a school activity, it is a life skill used in situations such as adding up items when shopping or paying a bill in a cafe.

The quick test of working memory is to say some numerals (at one-second intervals) and ask the student to repeat them in reverse order. For example, the tester says, 'Two, six, three.' And the subject should say, 'Three, six, two.'

Working memory scores are usually lower than STM scores, but if the difference is very noticeable, then the student will be handicapped in any mental activity in school, with consequent impact on classroom behaviour.

LONG-TERM MEMORY

I value Howard Gardner's (1999) theory of multiple intelligences (see Chapter 13). The theory of multiple intelligences is on my list of key theories for education. It explains why children often have great cognitive strengths accompanied by significant weaknesses. In particular, students with special needs rarely seem to have a uniformly performing intelligence for all activities and endeavours. I think the same theory applies to memory, especially for children with special needs and exemplified by the typical characteristic of an Asperger child to have impressive memory for a specific topic, yet weak recall abilities in other areas.

Curriculum content and structure in most subjects, if not all, still relies heavily on recall. This will have more impact on students with special needs than on other students. Again, it is worth bearing in mind that a poor long-term memory in one topic does not automatically mean a poor memory for all topics.

One of the best techniques for rote learning, for getting facts into long-term memory, is self-voice echo (see ARROW 2009). This technique, pioneered by Dr Colin Lane, involves learning from material recorded in your own voice. Many people learn material better when they hear material that they have recorded themselves.

SLOW PROCESSING

Students with special needs often process information more slowly than their peers. This deficit may be a major contributor to some of the classroom behaviours considered in this book. It is worth frequently reminding ourselves that some behaviours are a direct consequence of the special need. It will usually be easier for a teacher to adjust for this (and the other deficits mentioned in this chapter) than the student.

LEARNING STYLE

There is a range of advice on learning styles (see e.g. Mortimore 2003). Not all pupils will learn in the same way and there will be many factors that influence the efficacy of learning. One of the dangers that all students, but especially special needs students, face is global advice on learning strategies. For example, much as I admire and use mind maps (Buzan and Buzan 2000), I acknowledge that they do not appeal to nor work for everyone.

INFLEXIBILITY OF SUBSKILLS FOR MODIFICATIONS OR DEVELOPMENTS OF TASKS

Sometimes work in school curricula is structured to develop cognitively, building on previously mastered knowledge and concepts. It is possible to underestimate the impact of a development stage on a student.

I assessed a 12-year-old boy for maths difficulties. His mother (confirmed by the boy) said that one of his biggest difficulties was in doing subtraction problems, even those at the 28 – 19 level. When the boy added he used a discreet, fast and accurate counting-on strategy. Unfortunately he could not count backwards, so he could not reverse his strategy to perform subtraction. (His perception of subtraction was that he had to do the opposite of what he did for addition.) His school had organized for him to do a subtraction worksheet at the start of every maths lesson for ten weeks to give him practice in this operation. There was no improvement, because the prerequisite skill of counting backwards was not there and practice was not improving it. His problem was overcome by learning how to count on from the lower number. Sometimes intervention is about finding a method that is appropriate to the skills for the student while still achieving the learning objective. The potential for frustration and bad behaviour consequent on not being aware of development issues is high.

FREQUENT ABSENCE

The last item on the CBL refers to frequent absences from school. This situation can lead to underachievement and poor social integration.

MEDICAL CONDITIONS

For a student who has been diagnosed as having a neuro-behavioural condition, such as Tourette syndrome, or a medical condition, such as Prader-Willi syndrome, there is an additional challenge for teachers and adults. They have to decide if a behaviour is voluntary and thus controllable or a symptom of their medical condition.

CHAPTER 7

USING the CLASSROOM BEHAVIOURS LIST (CBL)

SCREENING FOR SPECIAL NEEDS

By combining the pattern of 'scores' (from a number of teachers and learning support assistants) on the Classroom Behaviours List for a pupil and checking against the lists of the characteristics of each special need (see chapter 4), it is possible to screen for an initial tentative identification of the special needs of a pupil who may be causing concern in the classroom.

It will enhance objectivity if copies of the Classroom Behaviours List can be given to several of the teachers and classroom assistants who work with the pupil for them to fill in *independently*. The blank template overleaf can be photocopied and used for this purpose. An informal 'average' can then be compiled and compared with the CBLs for each special need. If this comparison indicates a particular special need, then the characteristics of each special need as given in Chapter 2 can be used to provide further evidence for the screening process.

IDENTIFYING CONCERNS: A PUPIL'S CBL PROFILE

If a pupil is causing concern in a number of classes (or even one class) then the CBL can be given to all of his or her teachers for them to complete *independently*. The lists can then be compared to see the pattern of behaviours across the subjects, providing useful information for managing the pupil's behaviours consistently and encouraging teachers to share successful strategies.

Classroom behaviour	1	2	3	4	5
1. Slow to start work					
2. Refuses to do work					
3. Having the correct equipment					
4. Not starting work without individual instruction					
5. Completing written tasks					
6. Loses focus during tasks					
7. Accepting advice					
8. Accepting criticism from teacher					
9. Accepting criticism from peers					
10. Fiddles with pencils, multi-purpose tack … etc.					
11. Distracts other students					
12. Interferes with other students' work					
13. Persists with bad behaviour despite correction					
14. Makes inappropriate comments in class					
15. Withdraws quietly from task					
16. Does not seek help even when needed					
17. Displays sudden verbal outbursts					
18. Displays sudden physical outbursts					
19. Displays sudden emotional outbursts					
20. Leaves seat for no reason					
21. Unable to work on group tasks					
22. Is not accepted by peer group in class					
23. Is not accepted by peer group outside classroom					
24. Misinterprets instructions					
25. Misinterprets social communication					
26. Blames others for own difficulties					
27. Blames themselves for difficulties					
28. Believes they will fail on a task before starting					
29. Sets unrealistic goals for themselves					
30. Thinks they cannot improve/learn					
31. Unable to form friendships					
32. Limited participation in social activities					
33. Seems unhappy in class					
34. Absence from school					

USING THE CBL TO CREATE AN INDIVIDUAL BEHAVIOUR PLAN

The data from the CBLs for a student can be used to identify and then target specific behaviours, for example, in the sample CBL below compiled (and averaged from a number of teachers and support assistants) for a pupil who was causing concern, the seven highest rated behaviours have been starred (*) and could be selected for the first key targets for an individual behaviour plan for that student. These targets could also be identified for individual areas of the curriculum.

Classroom behaviour	1	2	3	4	5
1. Slow to start work				X	
2. Refuses to do work				X	
3. Having the correct equipment			X		
4. Not starting work without individual instruction				X	
5. Completing written tasks *					X
6. Loses focus during tasks *					X
7. Accepting advice				X	
8. Accepting criticism from teacher				X	
9. Accepting criticism from peers *					X
10. Fiddles with pencils, multi-purpose tack … etc.			X		
11. Distracts other students			X		
12. Interferes with other students' work		X			
13. Persists with bad behaviour despite correction				X	
14. Makes inappropriate comments in class		X			
15. Withdraws quietly from task *					X
16. Does not seek help even when needed *					X
17. Displays sudden verbal outbursts		X			
18. Displays sudden physical outbursts	X				
19. Displays sudden emotional outbursts				X	
20. Leaves seat for no reason				X	
21. Unable to work on group tasks				X	
22. Is not accepted by peer group in class			X		
23. Is not accepted by peer group outside classroom				X	
24. Misinterprets instructions		X			
25. Misinterprets social communication				X	
26. Blames others for own difficulties *					X
27. Blames themselves for difficulties	X				
28. Believes they will fail on a task before starting				X	
29. Sets unrealistic goals for themselves	X				
30. Thinks they cannot improve/learn *					X

31. Unable to form friendships				X	
32. Limited participation in social activities			X		
33. Seems unhappy in class				X	
34. Absence from school	X				

Of course, the number of targets selected will depend on a number of factors, including the level of intervention available, the time span, or the ability of the student to deal with a number of targets. The behaviours highlighted by the CBL can be categorized or grouped according to the nature of the behaviour. For example, the seven behaviours highlighted by the CBL above show a mixture of needs from the three categories (classroom management/personal organisation issues, social skills and communication issues, emotional support and guidance issues).

Because the CBL is structured around the behaviours of the pupil, it focuses on the needs of the pupil. These needs can then be addressed by interventions that should offer support in a way that is acceptable to the pupil. The interventions should include challenging the student's attributional style in order to build resilience and coping strategies (see Chapter 16). This implies involving the student in discussions about his or her behaviours.

After a period of intervention for the targets selected it is possible to re-evaluate using the CBL again to see if the areas of concern have reduced in score/severity, thus, hopefully, demonstrating the progress and efficacy of the interventions. Improvement, demonstrated and quantified by the CBL, will be important for future motivation.

If deemed appropriate, then some targets may be considered achieved and thus removed to be replaced by new targets. However, it may be that reducing the number of targets is the key objective initially. Introducing new targets too soon may make the student feel that improvement is not achievable. Attributional style (chapter 16) will play a part in addressing these issues.

If the CBL is completed by a number of teachers and/or learning support assistants then it may identify curriculum areas where the behaviours are more problematic. Again this supplies information to help with discussions with the student.

THE CBL AND 'STAFFING'

When I was head of a special school in Maryland, USA, I was introduced to the process of reviewing a student called 'Staffing'. It was not a unique procedure, but it was effective. We developed a structure which basically was a list of the areas which generally caused us concern and which we considered significant for progress in academic and affective issues. Any teacher or assistant who worked with the student was encouraged to contribute comments and insights. This simple process allowed everyone to hear each other's perceptions of the student. It also invariably led to a clear, useful and multifaceted picture of the student.

The structure of a Staffing would be dependent on the individual requirements of a particular school, but the CBL could be used to help structure the staffing of students by providing a starting framework for contributions and discussion. The CBL can also empower teachers to comment on a student's behaviours objectively.

CHANGES IN BEHAVIOURS

The CBL can be used to provide an initial evaluation of the pattern of behaviours of a particular student if staff think there is a sudden and inexplicable change in levels of behaviours. It is worth remembering that the pragmatic goal is to improve the student's behaviours, not implement a 'cure' for them.

THE 1–5 EVALUATION SCALE

Obviously the 1–5 evaluation scale is subjective. Different teachers will evaluate a similar level of behaviour differently. Over a period of time it may be possible to acknowledge these differences as the experience of the teacher or coordinator who collates the data grows. (If a number of teachers collate the data then they may have to meet to moderate the grades.)

CHAPTER 8

COMMON BEHAVIOURS across the SPECIAL NEEDS

There were ten behaviours rated with high levels of concern common across the first five special needs. These were:

1. Slow to start work

4. Not starting work without individual instruction

5. Completing written tasks

6. Loses focus during tasks

10. Fiddles with pencils, multi-purpose tack … etc.

16. Does not seek help even when needed

21. Unable to work on group tasks

25. Misinterprets social communication

28. Believes they will fail on a task before starting

32. Limited participation in social activities

The behaviours identified by teachers in the three participating countries as causing most concern for the first five special needs are, again, a mixture of the three categories, but are dominated by 'classroom management' with six of the ten classified as being in this category.

Classroom management is helped by consistency. Students with special needs appreciate consistency in structure, as do many students. A set routine for basic processes leaves more time for learning.

However, some classroom behaviours, for example 'having the correct equipment' (3) can cause angst in some teachers.

He is rarely properly prepared for the lesson, often forgetting essentials such as his exercise book or even a pen. (From a School Report on a 13-year-old ADHD boy)

The fact that the ten behaviours featured for the five special needs is a plus for classroom management, in that there should be significant benefits across the special needs when the behaviours are addressed.

CHAPTER 9

STRATEGIES from TEACHERS for the MAIN AREAS of CONCERN in CLASSROOM BEHAVIOURS as IDENTIFIED by the CBL

The teachers who completed the Classroom Behaviours List were also asked to share any strategies they had found successful for encouraging acceptable classroom behaviours. Their ideas are shared in this chapter. The six teachers from the 'Comenius Group' added further strategies.

Some of these strategies may be more appropriate for primary pupils aged 5–10 years and some may be more appropriate for secondary pupils aged 11–18 years. It is also important to remember that not every intervention will work with every pupil, and possibly not even for the same pupil in different circumstances or on different days, which is one of the reasons for listing a range of interventions.

Of course, this is not an exhaustive list. Also, many of the suggestions below may already be used routinely with pupils. Some may have slipped from use. This chapter should be considered as a working document, with any additional interventions added to the list and shared with colleagues working with these special pupils as each school builds its own 'toolbox' of interventions.

1. SLOW TO START WORK

- Make sure the pupil knows what the task involves, for example by making the instructions short, low stress and positive (and repeating them when necessary).

- Position the pupil close to the teacher to facilitate individual input at the beginning of the activity (but see next suggestion).
- Position the pupil at the back of the class if the intervention above makes the pupil feel uncomfortable or self-conscious, so that when the teacher (or learning support assistant) goes to help him or her, it is less obvious to other students.
- Make the pupil aware that he or she will be given extra time so that the task is not perceived as too daunting.
- Give the pupil a starting point so that he or she is ahead of others and is not afraid to make the first mark on the paper.
- Use the classroom assistant (if available) to check that the student has understood the task and that she knows where the task is heading and to create a plan.
- Encourage the pupil to do a mind map, a list or writing frame to get initial thoughts down on paper (find out which of these matches the pupil's learning style).
- Reward or acknowledge the effort made for first part of work being completed within a given time.
- Ensure that the task is at an appropriate level for the individual (should be an obvious consideration, but is not necessarily so) and that a specific, clear, manageable task is set.
- Allow use of information technology (IT) if this will overcome the fear of committing work to paper or let the student use a personal whiteboard where unwanted work can be easily erased.
- Use a buddy.
- Use a traffic light system …get ready, start… given visually as coloured prompts.

4. NOT STARTING WORK WITHOUT INDIVIDUAL INSTRUCTION

- Make sure the signal to start work is clear.
- Ensure that classroom management is consistent, structured and predictable.
- Make sure the pupil can read the instructions and/or understands the task. If reading is a problem then screen the pupil for print/paper colour contrast by trying coloured overlays.
- Get the pupil to reflect back or repeat the instructions.
- Ensure that the task is at an appropriate level for the individual, possibly starting with a task that is familiar to the pupil.

- Place the pupil in a group of pupils who do not have special needs where each pupil is given a different role in order to complete a given task.

- Encourage the student to believe that he or she will be able to succeed and reward him or her for the first part of work being completed within a given time (set an achievable starting target).

- Encourage the student to do a mind map or a writing frame to get initial thoughts down on paper.

- Lay out equipment ready for use to help the pupil focus on the task.

- Keep materials out of reach until the instructions are given, however, so that the pupil can focus on the instructions and not be distracted by fiddling with the materials.

- Make the pupil aware that he or she will be given extra time so that the task does not appear too daunting.

- Issue the pupil with a worksheet that has a summary of the expected task: colour coding and highlighting may help.

- Use differentiated material if appropriate, such as a labelled picture or a template to encourage success.

- Ensure that the task is not perceived as overwhelming or that the list of tasks is not too long and daunting.

- Encourage the pupil to verbalize his or her first sentence and then write it for them.

- Try to give the pupil some responsibility for starting.

- Give the pupil a personal audio recorder so he or she can record thoughts and ideas or use voice recognition software on a computer.

5. COMPLETING WRITTEN TASKS

- Position the pupil close to the teacher (or at the back of the class where help can be given discreetly) in order to give reminders to stay on task to read them unknown words.

- Provide IT with appropriate software *and training* if handwriting is a problem, so that the finished product is readable.

- Use a learning support assistant's support for drafting.

- Use writing frames or any form of scaffolding which is appropriate to the pupil.

- Give encouragement (realistic and genuine) at regular intervals. Encouragement from a teacher can aid a pupil towards completion of a given task, including praise, giving team points or other rewards.

- Remind the pupil about the time used and the time left without causing anxiety or pressure.

- Give breaks.

- Give the pupil cards (smiley faces) that he or she can display discreetly on the desk as a way of attracting support from the teacher or teaching assistant.

- Use mind mapping (see e.g. Buzan and Buzan 2000), which does not rely on sequential thinking.

- Remember that writing frames can aid the pupil towards completion of the task as they provide a structure. Also pupils are less likely to forget the points they want to make.

- Ensure that all tasks are of a suitable length for the pupil to complete or allow extra time for pupil to complete the task(s). The former is preferable as the time available for special needs pupils to do work is not infinite!

- Limit the space the pupil has to fill.

- Use different coloured paper for instructions and worksheets and for the pupil to write on. (Crossbow Education produce maths exercise books with coloured squared pages.)

- Colour code the instructions, using an agreed coding system.

- Use cloze procedures. Open-ended tasks are overwhelming for some pupils, for example, pupils who work sequentially and do not plan ahead.

- Minimize written work or allow pupil to record in different way, for example producing an audio record of the work, or voice recognition technology (make sure the student is trained) or by use of specifically prepared supporting worksheets.

- Reduce the number of requirements for the individual, then completion of a task should be more likely. For example, allow the pupil to concentrate on the flow of writing rather than worrying about spelling.

- Ensure that any reference material is available and accessible so that time is not wasted in searching.

6. LOSES FOCUS DURING TASKS

- Ensure the task is appropriate for the pupil.
- Break the task down into manageable chunks.

- Cover up the next step on the worksheet so the pupil can focus on the task in hand.

- Ensure that the tasks set have some variety, but are not confusing.

- Seat the pupil near the teacher so that regular reminders to stay on task, or praise for work attempted so far, can be given. Or seat the pupil in a less conspicuous place if the extra help makes the pupil feel self-conscious.

- Seat the pupil at the back of the class so that help can be given discreetly.

- Use a learning support assistant to refocus the pupil and discuss the next step required.

- Change the tone of your voice for different interactions with the pupil.

- Place a clock in front of the pupil as an aid to time focus. (However, this may not work with some pupils and may distract other pupils.)

- Keep the tasks short and change the activity regularly; this will help some pupils to concentrate.

- Allow short breaks.

- Move the pupil to a seat away from other pupils to aid concentration by minimizing distractions (maybe even a separate corral to provide a distraction free environment).

- Keep the classroom uncluttered (called a vanilla environment in the USA).

- Be aware that some pupils respond well to a competitive element to keep them focused, but others may find competition creates far too much anxiety.

- Give very explicit and appropriate targets. Check that what you, the teacher, judges as explicit is also perceived that way by the pupil.

- Use mind mapping and writing frames to help pupils to maintain focus as a structure is then in place. Also they are less likely to forget the points they wanted to make. The points can be made and recorded randomly, then placed in order later.

- Issue the pupil with a worksheet that has a summary of the expected task. Colour coding and highlighting may be appropriate to provide extra help and structure.

- Make sure that equipment to be used is easily available.

10. FIDDLES WITH PENCILS, BLU-TAK ... ETC.

- Ensure that the desk is free from clutter at the start of the lesson so that the temptation to fiddle is reduced.

- Remember that the use of IT will remove the need for other items to be on the desk and thus not be available to be fiddled with.

- Be aware that there may be times when it is better to allow a pupil to fiddle with something quiet, for example blu-tak, rather than allow them to distract others by a more intrusive activity.

- Place the pupil away from other pupils in order to reduce the distraction of others.

- Allow the pupil access to multi-sensory equipment so that he or she can fiddle productively!

- Give praise and reward for sitting still for an agreed length of time.

- Set achievable targets to encourage longer times on task.

- Insist that a pupil tidies up before commencing a new task to ensure that extraneous material is not left lying around to fiddle with.

- Accept the fact that different pupils have different learning styles.

- Avoid static learning and try to incorporate more kinaesthetic learning.

16. DOES NOT SEEK HELP EVEN WHEN NEEDED

- Place the pupil close to the teacher or learning support assistant so that it is possible for the teacher or LSA to check regularly and discreetly that the pupil is on task and understanding.

- Give praise and encouragement when the pupil is doing the work correctly so that it may be possible to build the confidence of the individual so he or she will ask for help when necessary.

- Help pupils to understand that mistakes can be an important part of the learning experience.

- Be accessible and non-judgmental (see Chapter 15 on Transactional Analysis).

- Create a classroom ethos where it is safe to ask questions.

- Create a positive learning environment (see Chapter 16 on attributional style).

- Give a positive response to pupils who ask for clarification (using both positive content and tone of voice).

- Set small targets to make it possible to ensure that the pupil is checked regularly.

- Encourage the pupil to appraise and evaluate his or her own work (this may need frequent monitoring) and to look for the next step in the work.

- Allow the learning support assistant to be close at hand to support the individual so that help can be given as soon as the individual reaches a hurdle or barrier.

- Understand that a pupil may be happier asking a friend to help with something he or she can't do and so some pupils could benefit from sitting next to a 'buddy' who is able to do the task (again this needs close monitoring so that the pupil and the buddy both benefit from the arrangement).

- Give the pupil a carefully individualized worksheet so that it may be possible for them to use this instead of having to seek help from the teacher.

- Give help very discreetly to those who do not wish to be seen needing or accepting help.

21. UNABLE TO WORK ON GROUP TASKS

- Place the child in a group with pupils who do not have special needs where each child is given a different role to help towards the completion of a given task so that they have their own role within the group.

- Watch and monitor group interactions and change group members when it is appropriate. Manage these changes empathetically.

- Give rewards to the group in order to encourage the pupil to work as part of the group.

- Start with paired activities with a particular friend or buddy who is willing to help.

- Give rewards to the student for displaying a positive attitude towards others.

- Introduce a social skills/competence programme to help address the areas that cause the difficulty.

- Allow the pupil access to a time-out room when he or she cannot handle the pressure.

- Investigate relationships with the peer group during Circle Time sessions. An LSA can be used in the group to encourage cooperation and to intervene when problems arise.

  Circle Time involves pupils sitting in a circle, exchanging ideas and feelings on a range of issues that are important to them, including behavioural and emotional issues. Through a range of activities positive behaviours are reinforced. …The very act of sitting in a circle emphasizes unity and equality and symbolically promotes the notion of equal responsibility. (Department for Education and Skills 2005)

25. MISINTERPRETS SOCIAL COMMUNICATION

- Ask pupils to repeat back their understanding of a conversation each time there is a problem so that they can be encouraged to respond appropriately next time.

- Encourage the pupil to ask people to repeat what they said (in a different way if possible, which requires staff training, a consistent attitude and an appropriate classroom ethos).

- Try to catch those moments when the pupil is responding appropriately and reward him or her appropriately.

- Investigate during Circle Time or group discussions how others view the pupil's reactions and encourage more appropriate responses.

- Use drama to give the opportunity for the pupil to try out different responses in the safe knowledge that they are less likely to upset or offend anybody.

- Use drama lessons or personal, social and health education (PSHE) lessons to make the pupil aware of the effect of facial expression, tone of voice and body language. It may be necessary to teach the pupil how to read the signs of non-verbal communication.

- Teach specific social skills, for example, how to interpret facial expressions.

- Don't use over-long or complex instructions.

- Be aware of pupils who interpret communications literally and teach them how to recognize alternative interpretations.

- Use agreed symbols rather than language for some instructions.

28. BELIEVES THEY WILL FAIL ON A TASK BEFORE STARTING

- Ensure that targets are small and achievable so that the pupil can receive regular praise for achievement during, as well as at the end of, the task.

- Give pupils a starting point for their work so that the first steps are taken for them.

- Provide a writing frame or introduce a structure of ever decreasing support as the pupil increases his or her independence.

- Encourage the student to mind map or create a writing frame so that his or her thoughts are quickly recorded and thus less likely to be forgotten.

- Recognize that working in a group can help if the student is given a specific role for part of the task so that he or she does not have to feel responsible for completing the whole task.

- Use group or paired reading to help a pupil feel that he or she can start a task.

- Reread a book that has already been read to pupils to give them the confidence to read it alone as they already have an understanding of the story, vocabulary and language involved.

- Reduce the pupil's timetable to enable him or her to feel able to cope with the remaining subjects.

- Give additional time to allow the pupil to start a task feeling more confident that he or she will finish the task.

- Build self-confidence by using appropriate praise. Praise the work, not the child: see attributional style (Chapter 16).

- Encourage positive thinking. Help build a positive attributional style (see Chapter 16).

32. LIMITED PARTICIPATION IN SOCIAL ACTIVITIES

- Encourage paired or group work in class, carefully selecting the other participating pupils.

- Give group rewards when a pupil is doing well to encourage others to feel more kindly towards this pupil.

- Give the pupil responsibility for looking after younger pupils in an area of strength in order to help the pupil in social time.

- Use buddies.

- Create the opportunity for the pupil to explain why he or she does not take part in social activities so that discussions can be structured appropriately.

- Allow pupil to stay in at break times with other pupils to play a game, use the computer or take part in some other appropriate reward.

- Investigate during Circle Time how others view the pupil's reactions and help him or her to create a more appropriate response.

- Give positive reinforcement for correct interactions with fellow pupils. Use appropriate praise!

A FINAL NOTE: CONSISTENCY

None of the suggestions outlined above will be as effective if they are not applied consistently and within a consistent framework (and ethos) for the student and for the class.

The following observation was taken from a report from Her Majesty's Chief Inspector of Schools on the subject of *Improving Attendance and Behaviour in Secondary Schools* (Office for Standards in Education (Ofsted) 2001). An extract is quoted below to emphasize the importance of consistency.

> The key to success when improving behaviour was the **consistency** with which staff, having agreed a policy, applied it. Pupils benefit if they know that the consequences of misbehaviour are the same wherever it takes place. This way, pupils will not circumvent rules and exploit differences in teachers' approaches. (Ofsted 2001, p.11)

Consistency is an especially important factor for pupils with special needs. They are often totally fazed by inconsistency or any change to routine. If a change in routine is planned then the adults involved should flag it up well ahead of time and do that several times as the change gets nearer, addressing the uncertainties and worries of the pupils concerned.

WHAT ARE THE FACTORS THAT MAY CONTRIBUTE TO A CLASSROOM BEHAVIOUR?

There may be a number of factors that contribute to a classroom behaviour. Some of the underlying concepts that contribute to communication, social competence and behaviours are discussed in later chapters in this book.

Some of the particular, single-cause factors are listed below:

- Inconsistent teachers: this could be the teacher who is everyone's friend one day and unapproachably strict the next. It could be the contrast between the teaching styles that a student meets in consecutive lessons and his or her inability to make the adjustment needed to cope with the change.

- Inappropriate teaching style such as the teacher talking for too long at one time.

- Inappropriate subject material: too difficult and over-challenging or too easy and patronizing.

- Inappropriate presentation of material, for example worksheets that are too busy or too crowded with information.

- Font colour or paper colour. Irlen syndrome or scotopic sensitivity can be addressed by using paper that is not white for worksheets.

- Inadequate differentiation for the pupil's special needs, such as not modifying the vocabulary and language in worksheets.

- External influences, for example, events at home, or in the playground.

- An inability in the pupil to self-evaluate and adjust behaviour.

- The pupil's underlying attitude or attributional style (see Chapter 16).

- Poor cognitive ability, needed to analyse a situation and respond appropriately.

- Environment, for example work in an uncluttered, tidy(ish) classroom. Research, reported in *The Times*, shows that we become antisocial when surrounded by decay and disorder (Ahuja 2009).

CHAPTER 10

The BENEFITS of DIFFERENT INTERVENTIONS

Many of the interventions suggested by the teachers in the survey and listed in Chapter 9 were similar irrespective of the special need of the individual. Most of the interventions fall into seven categories:

- Giving extra time to complete work.
- Considering where the student is placed in the classroom.
- Setting targets and giving praise and rewards for achieving the targets (thus influencing self-esteem, self-concept and attributional style).
- Using a learning support assistant to individualize intervention (discreetly and empathetically).
- Giving social skills and social competence training.
- Providing starting points and structure.
- Using information technology.

The benefits of each these interventions are discussed in more detail below.

GIVING EXTRA TIME TO COMPLETE WORK

Extra time is not an infinite commodity for a pupil and should be coordinated by all the teachers involved with the pupil who has special needs. By giving pupils extra time, various areas of concern are addressed:

- The completion of written tasks becomes more likely.
- Pupils are more likely to believe that they can achieve the given task.

- It will allow pupils to seek help without fear of being left behind.
- It allows time for the use of IT and appropriate software such as spell-check facilities.

Extra time can be taken during breaks or lunchtime if pupil and staff are willing. It should not be viewed or implemented as a punishment.

His class teacher, not appreciating the extent of the problem, allowed the class to leave the room to go to play once they had answered the questions correctly – my son didn't get any playtime. (Mother of a seven-year-old boy with dyslexia)

For some students a reduced timetable may be necessary to allow adequate time for key subjects, for example, it may be sensible for some dyslexic pupils to be 'disapplied' from taking a foreign language.

To reiterate, extra time needs to be managed and coordinated by all the teachers working with a particular pupil if it is to be efficacious. In order to make good use of the extra time, the student may need extra support and guidance, for example instruction on how to use voice recognition technology efficiently. Extra time needs to be productive, otherwise it will just mean extra time for frustration.

CONSIDERING WHERE THE STUDENT IS PLACED IN THE CLASSROOM

By placing the child near the teacher, or in a mutually agreed position in the classroom, it allows

- the teacher to refocus the child, discreetly, throughout the lesson
- one-to-one pertinent attention to be given in order to get the pupil started and then motivated during a given task
- disruption of other pupils in the class to be minimized.

By placing the child within a group of supportive peers it allows for

- group or paired reading and discussion to take place
- pupils to work cooperatively within a group where each individual takes a given role
- supportive peers to articulate their understanding of a topic (which can be a very effective learning experience for them, too).

SETTING TARGETS AND GIVING PRAISE AND REWARDS FOR ACHIEVING THE TARGETS

By setting short and achievable (achievable in the pupil's perception) targets, pupils will be

- encouraged to start on a given topic without feeling overwhelmed by the task in hand
- more likely to maintain concentration as the activity can be regularly reviewed and changed
- given more positive attention and feedback by the teacher which in itself will often be a reward.

Praise and reward from the teacher can come in many forms and will need to vary from pupil to pupil. Praising the work can be used to

- enhance the pupil's self-belief, confidence and attributional style
- reinforce appropriate behaviour
- help integration with other pupils (particularly by rewarding the group when the individual is doing well in a group task).

Praise is effective when it is given in the following circumstances:

- It is given for desirable behaviours or genuine accomplishment appropriate to the individual (remembering to praise the behaviour not the child).
- It is specific to the student's own accomplishments.
- It is expressed sincerely and realistically.
- It provides information to the pupil about the value of their accomplishments, thus helping them to self-evaluate more effectively (for example, 'I liked the way you used that word to give real interest to that opening sentence').

In John Hattie's (2009) book, *Visible Learning: A Synthesis of Over 800 Meta-analyses Relating to Achievement*, the most important influence on achievement is students' ability to accurately understand their own performance. However, 'expectations of success, which may be lower than students could attain, may create a barrier as students may only perform to whatever expectations they already have of their ability' (Hattie 2009, p.44). This conclusion is especially apposite for many of the students with special needs and their frequently observed low self-concept.

It attributes success to their efforts and ability, implying that they are able to achieve similar success in the future. Ultimately it encourages students to achieve for themselves rather than solely for the reward or just to please others, for example, the teacher or parent.

Rewards can come in many forms:

- stickers, house points, sweets, medals, trophies

- a choice of a fun activity – games, computer use, listening to music
- extra time for a break or preferred activity
- commendation in assembly or in a letter home to parents
- a group treat, for example, a trip out or watching a video
- being given the responsibility to help a teacher or take messages etc.

Caution: older students may actually wish not to be seen (by their peers) to get rewards. Some students may have their own 'quota' for praise. If that quota is exceeded then the praise may become counterproductive.

USING A LEARNING SUPPORT ASSISTANT TO INDIVIDUALIZE INTERVENTION (DISCREETLY AND EMPATHETICALLY)

If LSAs are available they can be used very effectively with an individual student to help with

- creating a plan to help students to organize their thoughts prior to starting work
- keeping a pupil focused by discussing the next step required after the first step has been completed
- giving reassurance when a task appears to be too difficult or demanding.

If the LSA is able to work with the individual within a group of peers it creates an ideal opportunity for the LSA to

- reinforce appropriate social communications
- make the student aware of non-verbal communications within the group
- intervene as soon as problems arise so that the pupil does not become agitated and upset.

GIVING SOCIAL SKILLS AND SOCIAL COMPETENCE TRAINING

Through provision of social skills training a student can become more integrated into social groups and relate more successfully to adults.

- The student is less likely to offend his or her peers.
- The student is less likely to upset a teacher or other adults.
- Specific communication issues can be addressed.
- Self-esteem should be raised.
- The student should be able to appraise and self-monitor the reactions consequent on his or her own actions.

By providing training that integrates social skills into a social competency, students can learn to

- interact more successfully with peers and adults
- adjust their responses to new situations so that they are appropriate to the stimuli received
- raise their self-esteem and self-concept
- reduce the frequency of conflicts with peers and adults.

PROVIDING STARTING POINTS AND STRUCTURE

By giving a student a starting point, a range of difficulties can be overcome:

- A student will be more likely to start on the task as he or she is not faced with a blank page.
- Individual instruction may be less necessary if an activity is clearly set out or possibly structured when it is given to the student.
- Completing a task in a given time can be made to appear more possible if the student has a head start.
- The structure of a writing frame allows pupils to get their ideas down onto paper and provides a secure reference so that they are less likely to forget their original ideas.
- If a student is given a role within the group that matches his or her capabilities, that role can enable the student to feel worthwhile and needed.

USING INFORMATION TECHNOLOGY

IT support can provide a student with a learning difficulty a much-needed means of communication at a standard that matches their aspirations and ability. It is not sufficient to just supply the hardware and software. Training and practice are essential.

The benefits include the following points:

- A word processor can enable a student to produce a piece of work that looks neat.
- The student can have the confidence to commit work to a screen knowing that it will not make a mess if he or she wants to change and edit the work.
- Voice output software can make a poor reader more independent.
- The spell-check facility enables students who do not spell well to produce a more accurate piece of work. (There are some very

sophisticated spell-check programs available, many involving voice output and speech recognition.)

- Voice-input/speech-recognition software enables pupils with extreme difficulties with writing and spelling to get their thoughts down onto paper, hence removing some of the frustrations these pupils face.

- IT can help with keeping a student on task.

If the teacher is using an interactive whiteboard or computer based presentation, it should be possible to provide the student with a copy of the material presented in the lesson to be used as ready-made notes. This can be provided, preferably for editing and for using reading technology, electronically (software specialists for special needs are Iansyst: see www. iansyst.co.uk).

CHAPTER 11

The PUPILS' OWN VIEWS

The usefulness of the strategies described in Chapter 10 is reinforced by the views of dyslexic pupils who were 'included' in a north Somerset comprehensive school (Thomson and Chinn 2001). The students were asked to suggest ways that teachers could help them in school. Although the advice comes from students with dyslexia, much of that advice is relevant to other special needs. Their suggestions form the headings, and the comments on each suggestion are mine.

THINGS THAT HELP

Help being given quietly and discreetly to individuals

It is worth noting that whenever or whatever help is given, if that help is not given empathetically then it may not be received positively, or any academic gain will be outweighed by loss of self-esteem. It may also result in a student not asking for help in the future.

Being given more time

This assumes that the student is ready to give more time (often a school day is far more tiring for special needs students).

Having handouts to summarize work

This eliminates or reduces the need for note taking and gives the student an accurate record of the work (for review or for revision). It also increases the chances of the student paying attention to what is being said. The act of note taking often requires so much effort that the student is unable to focus on both the listening and the writing. Not every pupil can dual task.

Marking work in dark colours tidily

This reduces the impact of negative feedback. Few people enjoy the experience of being told they are wrong, even though coping with negative feedback is a life skill. The way we are told we are wrong can be destructive. Some control on the impact could be achieved by using a less strident colour than red or by reducing the number of negative comments or by adding in some positives.

I saw a student's maths exercise book when he came for interview for a place in my school. There was a maths exercise he had done. He had done 12 questions and had ten ticks and two crosses and a score of 10/20, with no comment from the teacher. I was puzzled as I could not understand the marking scheme. For example, two marks per question would give 20/24. I asked the student to explain. He said that there were 20 questions, but he had only had time to do 12. A positive comment from the teacher might have improved motivation. The idea of not using red pens for marking received some bad press from some (predictable) newspapers who did not fully grasp the reasoning behind the suggestion.

Praise

Praise, if not patronizing, is a great morale booster and motivator (by no means exclusive to special needs students in that effect). Praise is usually associated with success and differentiating work so that special needs students can experience meaningful success is good inclusive practice. It is important to praise the work and not the child's intelligence in order to protect self-esteem. This is another idea that has received negative comments from the less considered newspaper writers. If you do not understand the principle, you should be cautious about making vigorous comments.

Working in smaller groups

A smaller group should result in more teaching and guidance time for the student. However, the group has to have the right composition. Group dynamics will be a critical factor, for example, placing a motivated dyslexic student in a high level disruptive group may not improve the quality of teacher–student interaction. Although this book emphasizes the many common characteristics of different special needs, it does not advocate all and any mix of special needs in one group.

Trained teachers who are aware of difficulties they face and teachers who care

Students know when a teacher has the skills to help them. Students also sense the empathy of adults around them. For subjects such as English and mathematics, the training should be well beyond mere awareness. There is a strong case for a whole school awareness to cover all subjects coupled with an understanding of how a special need will impact on each subject. I maintain that awareness of the learning needs of special needs pupils will help teachers be more effective with all students. The specific deficits of the special needs population are not exclusive to them.

A 15-year-old girl with significant special needs found games and physical education a problem. She suffered from monocular vision, poor balance, low muscle tone, poor stamina and a need to visit the toilet often. After a very hesitant participation in games activities she was punished by being made to walk around the hall for the duration of her mid-morning break. The school had a strong reputation for special needs...on paper. Provision has to be real, not just on paper.

Grades that show individual improvements

Schools may, understandably, present achievement and effort grades on the same report. However, for the special needs student who makes huge efforts for small gains may not find the comparison of the two grades motivating. Communication strategies are not always universally applicable.

Work being judged for content, not spelling

It is not just having the spelling marked as wrong that is the problem. It is pupils restricting the vocabulary they use to the words they think they can spell rather than using their true range of vocabulary. Even using the words they think they can spell does not guarantee accuracy! One consequence of this restricted vocabulary is that the work produced may look immature. It may then receive a low grade that may well add to demotivation for that student.

There is also the possibility of another factor affecting the standard of work. Many students with special needs find dual tasking very difficult, so, by concentrating on spelling, creativity is depressed, or if creativity takes over, spelling becomes inaccurate.

One of the teachers of English (Malcolm Litten) at Mark College asked all 80 pupils at the college to spell 'dyslexia'. He received 70 different spellings.

Access to catch-up exercises

This is such a good idea. It should be obvious, of course, but then the obvious can be overlooked. If a school is to become special needs friendly, then having a range of resources for catch-up is an essential requirement, for example a collection of flash cards that can be selected for individual needs. It could be a CD-ROM of key information, which will be especially useful if the colours and font sizes can be changed. Again, we need to remember that time is not infinite and that many special needs pupils are tired enough just coping with a normal length of day.

Teachers not going too fast

Often students with special needs are slow processors, write slowly, are slow to organize themselves and have memory problems if too much information comes in at one time.

THINGS THAT DON'T HELP

Their observations about what *doesn't* help included the following items.

Teachers who go too fast

See above!

Being expected to produce the same amount of work in the same time as non-dyslexic peers

Expectations can motivate or demotivate. Often the different outcome is down to a very small difference in the expectation and how it expressed and evaluated. Students with special needs tend not to work as quickly as their peers. This not a consequence of being 'a bit slow' which infers a low IQ. Speed of working is not a function of IQ, but of such factors as reading skills, writing speed or spending time thinking of an alternative word that can be spelled correctly.

A 300-word essay from a dyslexic student may be the outcome of much more blood, sweat and tears than a 1000-word essay from a non-dyslexic peer.

The CBL includes behaviours involving speed, such as 'slow to start work'. Speed is an issue in many classrooms. (Chapters 9 and 10 offer ideas)

Teachers who do not stick to the point and over-stretch pupils' short-term memory

When a student has a short-term memory deficit, especially if exacerbated by the need to recall information in a correct sequence, then the last thing needed is for a teacher to go off at a tangent. Clear, focused information, presented at a sensible pace and presented visually and orally is of benefit to all students, but essential for those with special needs. Sometimes starting with a preview and ending with a review is a great help.

Teachers who know that pupils are dyslexic, but do not help them (but not being patronized)

Some teachers won't help. Some say they don't believe in dyslexia or dyspraxia or ADD. Sadly that attitude can be found in any education sector. Sometimes perfect people find it hard to believe that others may have imperfections.

The issue of help is about balance and constantly adjusted balance. One of the goals of special education is to reduce the dependency on help when it is appropriate to do so. Certainly help must never be perceived as patronizing.

Too much copying from the board and teachers who clear the board too soon

I could add, with some personal embarrassment, 'teachers with poor handwriting'. I once taught a pupil with a short-term memory that allowed him to copy just one letter at a time from the board. He would look up at the board, look down at the page, write a letter, look back at the board, hoping to find the right place and so on. It was a devastating handicap. Ready-made notes would have made such a difference to his life. Even copying from a book or worksheet where the refocusing is closer is a slow process for some students.

Usually the issue of awarding extra time for examinations is far less contentious than it was in the 1980s.

Having test results read out loud

Often a special needs student has fragile self-esteem, eroded by years of negative feedback. For that feedback to be so publicly revealed is an additional insult to the injury of knowing that you do not do well with tests.

Being told off when a pupil is asking a friend for help

This is a good example of an understandable, but inappropriate response from a teacher. A greater awareness of the potential benefit of a 'buddy' could turn a negative into a positive in that it gives responsibility to two students. For some special needs students, being able to ask someone for help in remembering instructions is a survival skill (as ever a balance is needed less this become a manifestation of helplessness).

Confusing dyslexia with stupidity

Despite many years of experience of work with students with specific learning difficulties, I could still be shocked by the appearance of a piece of written work from the student with whom I had just had an intellectually stimulating conversation. If I judged the student by the written work alone, I might assume he or she was less than bright. It can be easy to judge incorrectly on the basis of too little evidence.

Being made to read aloud in class (or spell a word)

This has to be the ultimate in lack of awareness and empathy, yet I know it still happens. I recently worked in Australia, where a lecturer told me of a game played in classrooms. The children become 'gunfighters' who have to be 'quick on the draw' in knowing times table facts. The teacher shouts out a fact and the first child to answer has 'shot' the other child out of the competition. Not a good game for slow processors.

Public failure is not beneficial for self-esteem. It is not difficult to recognize when an activity is discriminatory. One of the most moving recollections of school I have ever read is the following, which was given to me by a Danish friend, recalling her maths lessons:

I am sitting in my room looking at the open maths book, getting ready to do my homework. All I can see are the numbers on the paper, numbers that frighten me and make me sad.

I keep sharpening my pencils again and again, constantly writing and erasing my answers making the pages in my maths book unreadable.

Most of the pages are full of my teacher's red and blue notes. Everything I have written has been wrong.

The teacher's comments are filling as much space as are my attempts to please him and live up to his far too high expectations. I know that tomorrow I will again have to face humiliation in the classroom.

He will look at our homework and ask me questions he knows I cannot answer. I will try to make myself invisible again, but he will find me, asking me another impossible question. Everyone will look at me and he will say loudly, 'Let's ask someone who will know the answer.'

It is not what he is saying that hurts me, but it is his harsh voice, his hostile body language and angry expressions, his cold, staring eyes, his angry stamping on the floor, his way of saying my name, his tight angry lips, the hard finger poking my back while he yells out loud, blaming me for not being able to do mathematics.

It is worth noting that whenever or whatever help is given, if that help is not given empathetically then it may not be received positively or any academic gain will be outweighed by loss of self-esteem. It may also result in a student not asking for help in the future.

PART TWO

SOME RELEVANT THEORIES

CHAPTER 12

SOCIAL SKILLS, SOCIAL COMPETENCE and SPECIAL NEEDS

In Chapter 3 the behaviours (13 out of 34) from the Classroom Behaviours List that reflect problems with social skills and communication issues were listed as follows:

9. Accepting criticism from peers

11. Distracts other students

12. Interferes with other students' work

13. Persists with bad behaviour despite correction

14. Makes inappropriate comments in class

17. Displays sudden verbal outbursts

21. Unable to work on group tasks

22. Is not accepted by peer group in class

23. Is not accepted by peer group outside classroom

25. Misinterprets social communications

26. Blames others for own difficulties

31. Unable to form friendships

32. Limited participation in social activities

These behaviours make a significant contribution to the concerns expressed by teachers.

It seems reasonable to expect that children will develop social skills. It is more debatable as to the extent of the role of schools in helping to develop these skills. Certainly it should not be expected to be the sole responsibility of schools. Whatever the outcome of that debate, it seems to be accepted and right that schools must contribute to the development of these skills if only to improve behaviour and behaviours. The UK government offered the SEAL (Social and Emotional Aspects of Learning) guidance in 2005 (see DfES 2005).

There is evidence that children with special needs are more vulnerable to the negative influence of the link between repeated failure and social and emotional problems.

In Hattie's 2009 book *Visible Learning*, which researched what factors improve achievement in schools, he found that, 'The relationship of self-efficacy, self-concept, aspects of motivation and persistence with achievement are among the larger correlates' (p.45). He also notes that, 'Whereas cognitive ability reflects what an individual can do, personality traits reflect what an individual will do' (ibid.).

This chapter overviews some of the implications of social skill training for children with learning difficulties. There is an overlap, an interaction and an interdependency between many of the concepts that influence the affective domain. Some of these interrelationships (for example, multiple intelligences and social competence) are illustrated in the following chapters. Social skills and social competence depend on many factors. They cannot be taught without an awareness of these other factors.

SOCIAL SKILLS AND SOCIAL COMPETENCE

First, we should understand what 'social skills' means. There is a significant difference between social skills and social competence.

Social skills are the specific behaviours (somewhat akin to the classroom behaviours) that enable a person to communicate and respond effectively with others. These skills can be learned for given circumstances and scenarios but *social competence* is achieved only if a pupil can perform these social skills in a smoothly flowing sequence and adapt them effectively for non-rehearsed and unfamiliar situations (somewhat akin to classroom behaviour).

Hence any child who is over-literal in his or her application of social knowledge and skills will be at a disadvantage, as will the child who seeks absolute consistency and certainty in everything. The development of social competence is at a far higher cognitive level (for example, see Bloom's (1956) taxonomy) than learning social skills.

Social skills and social competence will help a pupil integrate with his or her group. This in turn will help self-esteem, and will also open the way for more peer support. One of the objectives of an inclusive classroom should be to open as many avenues of support as are possible and that are acceptable to the pupil with special needs. If nothing else, this gives the pupil some sense of control over where the support comes from. Meaningful inclusion depends on acceptance.

The effective use of social skills, social competence, relies on a range of aptitudes that require cognitive ability. Social skill training programmes require that the student has to be able to

- identify situations in which a social behaviour is appropriate
- select the appropriate skills to be used in a given situation
- recognize that situations that appear similar may not be
- perform these skills fluently in appropriate combinations according to the social standards acceptable to the group
- recognize and adjust to the different social standards of different groups
- accurately perceive the other participants' verbal and non-verbal cues
- flexibly adjust to acknowledge these cues.

These make up the common sequence of actions of most social skills teaching programmes. The pupil has to be able to

- analyse the situation
- generate alternative reactions
- appraise these reactions
- implement the most effective social skill.

That is a highly complex sequence of thoughts and draws on many subskills and experiences. This is not to say that teachers should not try to teach these skills, but teachers have to be aware that the learning process may take some time for some pupils. Expectations should be appropriate to the child's cognitive abilities in this domain without compromising the ultimate objectives and goals.

Let us consider some of the subskills needed to succeed in this four-step social skills sequence.

Analyse the situation

If the situation is not unique to the student then he or she needs to be able to recall a similar situation. If it is unique then the student has to relate it to a previous situation that is as similar as possible.

The student has to identify the key pertinent issues. Then the student may need to interpret the non-verbal components of the situation, for example, facial expressions, voice tone and body language. These may significantly modify the initial interpretation of the situation. None of these interpretations are simple, for example the way people smile can mean different things. Smiling is not just an upward turn of the mouth and a flash of the teeth (though many politicians think this is enough when trying to convince us that they are so likeable).

There could also be a need to appraise the impact of the context on the situation if it is different from a previous experience. And all this may have to be done quickly, which is not good news if the student is a slow processor. Social interactions often move along and evolve rapidly. It is easy for a student with special needs to be judged and dismissed as 'slow'.

Generate alternative reactions

Not everyone is a natural flexible thinker and thus may not be able to generate alternative reactions. Even if alternatives can be generated, each extra interpretation will require evaluation and the effort involved may be resisted and will certainly take time.

Appraise these reactions

Again quick interpretation is needed and possibly adjustments to take into account those reactions. This appraisal also demands an ability to project and get into others' minds, to understand others and to realize that they might not have same motivations or goals.

All the skills from the first step are needed again, including non-verbal communication receptive skills. If the social interaction is with a group, then the student needs to be able to identify who the key people are and prioritize appraising their reactions. There will be a range of reactions and the student will need to be able to prioritize and identify the key reactors.

Implement the most effective social skill

This requires good and quick decision-making and all that entails. There then has to be instant and ongoing responsive adjustment.

At a higher level of competence the student may be able to structure his or her initial response to 'test the water'. The impact and the reactions have to be appraised and evaluated objectively. This has to be done from others' perspectives, too.

Four subskills affecting communication

Spence (1995) draws attention to the four subskills that affect communication:

- Reception ability: the ability to be, and remain, switched on to the right wavelength, to listen, to look, to receive the messages sent out by others.

- Interpretative ability: the ability to interpret accurately the message which another person is sending, what he really means, what he really wants.

- Responsive ability: the ability to decide on and adopt appropriate reactions – to meet another's need. It involves decision-making, evaluation, the use of reason as well as psychological awareness.

- Message ability: the ability to translate appropriate reactions into clearly transmitted unambivalent messages.

It seems reasonable to speculate that students on the autism spectrum and those with ADHD are likely to find these subskills challenging, but for different underlying reasons.

Interpersonal and intrapersonal intelligence

Two of Howard Gardner's (1999) multiple intelligences are pertinent to social skills and competence. *Interpersonal intelligence* is about a person's capacity to understand the intentions, motivations and desires of other people. While this is an important intelligence for students, it is an especially important one for teachers. Much of the work on behaviours will rely on this intelligence being well developed in teachers and tutors to counterbalance the deficits in some special needs students if nothing else. *Intrapersonal intelligence* is about understanding oneself, which is also highly influential in the communications that support social interactions. Part of the attraction of Gardner's theory for me as a teacher is that it explains that intelligence is not one homogenous entity, but that people have areas of relative strength and weakness.

A pupil can be involved in a social skills training programme as part of PSHE lessons using, for example, Social and Emotional Aspects of Learning (SEAL: DfES 2005), Social Skills Training (Spence 1995) or Circle Time activities (Circletime 2009). Issues can be explored through drama or PSHE without them having to be identified as a particular need for a particular individual. If a specific target has been identified from the CBL, then all teachers and learning support assistants can, without overwhelming the pupil with input, provide positive (and appropriately acceptable) guidance.

Some pupils may be able to learn and be reasonably competent at selecting the correct social response for a given situation but they may still not be able to adjust their selection responsively or they may not be able to blend their new social skills into social competence. Both these abilities require a level of empathy and cognitive skill that might not be available to them. The six special needs covered in this book will have vastly different levels of skill and success with social competence. For example, many of the dyslexic students I have met have excellent social skills, whereas the students with ADHD are often too overwhelmed by impulsivity to function effectively, consistently or sensitively.

MORAL DEVELOPMENT

There are many other concepts that have been promoted as having an influence on social competence. These could be considered, even if some are currently less fashionable educationally. It may be useful to refer back to obtain a different perspective on the complex area of social competence without waiting for the inevitable return swing of the education pendulum to sweep up 'old' theories again at some point in the future.

For example, Kohlberg's stages (see Wilson, Williams and Sugarman 1967, p.270) of moral development, which have a distinctly Piagetian flavour, look at how a social interaction may depend on the moral developmental stage of the pupil. As many pupils with special needs exhibit cognitive immaturity, then it may be that they will find some of the more complex actions and reactions very difficult to understand and implement.

Spence (1995) discusses developmental considerations which tally closely with Kohlberg's thoughts. She notes, for example, that the early stages of social development are characterized by egocentricism, which is equivalent to Kohlberg's pre-moral level.

While Kohlberg's stages are developmental, he emphasizes the ability of people to regress to any or all of the previous stages in some situations. An illustrative example of this is driving a car. At the pre-moral level, the driver drives as though he is the only person on the road, probably fast and motivated only by his own need for pleasure. At the next level, the driver, rushing along the motorway at 90 mph, slows down to 70 mph when he sees the police car ahead. At the conventional role conformity level, the driver keeps to the speed of the majority of other, law-abiding drivers around him. And at the highest level he drives at a safe and responsible speed, because that is the right thing to do.

This construct, particularly where the realization that a person can regress to lower levels of motivation and response, provides another facet in the understanding of the reactions of students with special needs in different circumstances.

Kohlberg's stages of moral development

1. Pre-moral level
    Self-centred
    Conforms to obtain rewards

2. Authority influences
    Rules are obeyed to avoid punishment

3. Conventional role conformity
    Conforms to obtain peer approval

4.   Individual principles
       Self-regulation
       Awareness of the rights (and needs) of others.

(Wilson *et al.* 1967, p.270)

One cause of a classroom behaviour may be that the pupil is operating at the lowest level of moral development and therefore will do a task only if he or she anticipates a material reward rather than operating at a higher level of moral development and thus being aware that a more appropriate behaviour might be to just do the right thing. As with so many aspects of education the process of addressing this issue is developmental, though not necessarily in a rigid Piagetian fashion.

Students may have to be initially taught at their developmental stage, with the instruction leading them to develop the subskills they need to progress to higher stages.

In an example of a misinterpretation of behaviour, a 14-year-old student with Prader-Willi syndrome (PWS) was walking past a drinks dispensing machine in school, during an activities week when rules were somewhat more relaxed. Displaying one of the characteristics of a PWS child, she decided she wanted a drink and headed for the machine, a coin at the ready. The LSA asked her to stop. She didn't. The LSA told her to stop. She didn't. The LSA stood in front of the machine. The child pushed her aside and was accused of assault by the school. One of the, sadly, uncontrollable impulses of a PWS child is a fixation and overwhelming impulse to obtain food. In effect, without the ability to control her reactions, the student was operating at level one, making the LSA's choice of intervention totally inappropriate. The student was punished. The school was vulnerable to accusations of inappropriate accommodation for a disability.

Regressions to lower stages are not always the consequence of a medical condition that creates a hormonal surge. Regression could be the consequence of drugs or alcohol, or of a recent interaction outside the classroom.

CHAPTER 13

MULTIPLE INTELLIGENCES

Let me explain why Howard Gardner's (1999) theory of multiple intelligences is one of my key theories for understanding special needs. I shall start by looking at the potential problems of 'intelligence testing'.

Intelligence is a concept to be taken with caution. For example, as soon as someone describes a politician as 'very intelligent' I feel scepticism about the concept of intelligence. I extend this cynical attitude to intelligence testing. Back in the 1960s when Russia was a communist country, Soviet psychologists had an 'unconditionally negative regard' for psychometrics as a science (Krutetskii 1976, p.12). They felt that intelligence tests served the class aims of the bourgeoisie. I am not quite that far down the line of idealism. My concern is that intelligence tests are not always appropriate for students with some special needs. Sometimes people's interpretations of the 'intelligence' measured by such tests lead to expectations that may be unrealistic. However, that is not to say that these tests do not have a place in special needs education and provision, even if that place comes with a 'use with caution' label.

For a while in the 1980s some educators looked for the ACID profile in the subtests of the Wechsler Intelligence Scale for Children (WISC). This idea was based on the 'spiky' profile of performance of a student on the subtests that make up the Wechsler Intelligence Scale. Dyslexic students would often underperform on four of the subtests: Arithmetic, Coding, Information and Digit Span. While this interpretation would be considered unsophisticated now, it was innovative at the time in that it drew attention to uneven performances in intelligence tests. It recognized that children do not have the same levels of ability in all skills. One of the key contributing causes to the ACID profile was the poor short-term memories of dyslexic students.

The understanding we can draw from this is that a low score in a test may not be an accurate measure of ability. The measure may be unduly influenced by a deficit in a subskill, such as memory. There can be some confusion between memory and intelligence, for example the BBC television quiz game *Eggheads* is largely a test of memory rather than intelligence. The same argument could be applied to the skill of spelling and those who think that good spelling is an indication of intelligence.

Sir, 'Purrfect spelling' (leading article, June 24) attracts an unjustified arrogance from those who are blessed with the specialized memory that can achieve this outcome.

Perfect spelling is not a consequence of higher intelligence. It is not that type of skill. It requires a perfect category of memory that can accurately visualize the way that a word is written. There may be some patterns and spellings that can be related back to Latin or Saxon, but the relationships and patterns are not consistent enough for these to be reliable deductive procedures.

Good spelling is primarily a feat of memory and should not bestow upon those who can demonstrate the skill any intellectual superiority over those who cannot, especially those with dyslexia. S.J. Chinn. (Letter to , 1 July 2006)

Gardner's theory of multiple intelligences presents a much broader picture of intelligence. In his first book, Gardner proposed seven separate intelligences:

- linguistic
- logical-mathematical
- musical
- bodily-kinaesthetic
- spatial
- interpersonal
- intrapersonal.

When we take this theory and apply it to special needs, it can explain some of the inconsistencies in the abilities of students with special needs, as well as those with no identified special needs. It is sometimes assumed, for example, that dyslexic people are naturally creative and have high spatial and bodily-kinaesthetic intelligences. This is true of some, but not true of all. Some anecdotally link Asperger syndrome with logical-mathematical intelligence. Again this is an over-generalization.

Linguistic and logical-mathematical intelligences are the intelligences that are most valued in schools. It happens that these are the two intelligences most likely to be depressed by special needs. Dyslexia, for example, affects linguistic achievements, especially as traditionally measured by schools, that is, by writing. It also can affect mathematics.

Interpersonal intelligence is a weakness for many students on the autistic spectrum. The concept of 'intelligence' as a summary of a person's abilities and potential is unproductive. It can easily lead to inaccurate and unrealistic expectations. Students with special needs are especially susceptible to such limiting expectations.

These are important implications of Gardner's theory, not least because they imply the possibility of strengths alongside weaknesses. A focus on strengths can give students an experience of success, which may well counter some of their negative experiences. One of my former students explained to me one day just how important playing football (soccer) was to him. He said that without that release and the feelings of capability it gave him, he would simply not cope with classroom work. Gardner's theory links to self-esteem and self-concept. At the obvious level of correlation, it explains why depriving a student with special needs of the activity he or she likes may have a far more negative influence than expected. It is also likely that the student's behaviour in the next lesson may be set in place before the student enters the classroom.

Multiple intelligences theory also links to social competence. If a student has low interpersonal intelligence, he or she will be handicapped when learning social skills and competence. Learning social competence may take more time and may need a different approach for such students.

CHAPTER 14

SELF-ESTEEM and SELF-CONCEPT

During my 24 years as a head of schools for special needs pupils, I gained significant experience of Statements of Special Educational Needs. A Statement of Special Educational Needs was a document about the pupil. It was constructed to include a list special needs and a set of objectives designed to meet the pupil's special needs. One objective that occurred quite frequently was, 'Improve his/her self-esteem.' Of course, this is a laudable objective. Many pupils with special needs have low self-esteem, but the Statement rarely gave any indication as to how this was to be achieved for the pupil, how it would be monitored and measured, what would be a suitable measure of improvement or indeed what was understood by self-esteem.

Lawrence (1996), an educational psychologist with a good understanding of and empathy for dyslexia, linked self-esteem to self-concept, self-image and ideal self, with self-concept as the umbrella term.

He defined *self-concept* as the sum total of an individual's mental and physical characteristics and his or her evaluation of them. Self-concept is the individual's awareness of him- or herself. Lawrence (1996) suggested that self-concept develops in three areas:

- self-image
- ideal self
- self-esteem.

He then defined these three terms:

- *Self-image* is the individual's awareness of his or her mental and physical characteristics.
- *Ideal self* is the collection of ideal characteristics the individual should possess.
- *Self-esteem* is the individual's evaluation of the discrepancy between self-image and ideal self.

I recall being horrified to see the legend on the back of a T-shirt worn by a boy whose self-esteem was extremely fragile. The legend read, 'Remember, second is the first loser.' 'Where did you get that from?' I asked. 'From my Dad.'

Lawrence's definitions clarify why so many children (and adults) with special needs have a problem with low self-esteem. They are surrounded by external expectations and experiences that help create the collection of characteristics they desire for their ideal self and yet they receive many negative experiences and feedback that depress self-esteem without sufficient positive experiences with which to build the resilience that helps form a strong self-image. The influence of experiencing meaningful success cannot be underestimated. It would be impossible to quantify this and say how much meaningful success and across how many areas it is needed, but some special needs pupils get very little at all.

A factor that can have a great influence on self-concept is expectations. Expectations can have a powerful effect, positive or negative, on self-concept, self-image and self-esteem. A student is subject to expectations from a variety of sources and the extent of the influence from a particular source can vary according to the pupil's age or circumstances. Expectations can come for parents, teachers, learning support assistants, peers, siblings, community, culture, media, grandparents and, increasingly, government. Not only will these expectations shape self-esteem, self-concept and self-image, but also the inevitable inconsistency of expectations emanating from so many sources will create extra pressures and confusions for the student.

Expectations can transform success, or the perception of success, into failure, and vice versa.

When I was the principal of the school I had founded, it had a strong reputation for improving the self-esteem and self-concept (see Burden 2005) of its students. Indeed one of the local education authority (LEA) representatives who was charged with monitoring our provision for students from his LEA told me, 'The trouble with you and your school is that you give your pupils far too much self-esteem.' Now, although that could be viewed as a preposterous statement, there could be an argument for not overdeveloping self-esteem in isolation. A psychologist on one of my maths learning disabilities training courses smiled as I told the story of 'too much self-esteem' and said, 'You know, psychotics have too much self-esteem!' (When you think of how the bad guys in movies are often portrayed, you can see the relationship.) The argument is not that my school could be producing an alumni of psychotics, but that self-esteem should be grounded in reality. A student with 'too much' self-esteem could be very vulnerable when faced with failure.

There should be a broader construct than self-esteem that should lead to a broader objective, which is why I was so attracted to the concept of attributional style (see Chapter 16). Attributional style allows for interventions that are far more targeted at the developmental needs of the student and, most importantly, teach how to deal with adversity and challenges. The links here are to social skills, motivation and resilience. Raising self-esteem does not teach students how to deal with adversity; indeed it may do just the opposite, in that a failure may have a catastrophic effect on self-esteem, leaving students feeling helpless, or the students may avoid any risk which they judge will damage their self-esteem.

THE VICIOUS CIRCLE OF SELF-FULFILLING INABILITY

Pupils who constantly experience failure can find themselves in a vicious circle of self-fulfilling inability and helplessness. Some children choose an escape strategy, avoidance, in order to avoid their self-predicted disappointment. Some pupils have an internal resource bank of emotional information based on previous experiences of failure. Since negative information tends to dominate it can take the student to initiate avoidance, thus overriding any involvement in the task and making the student resistant to the teacher's encouragement.

For these students, the initial emotion-based reaction on seeing a challenging task is, 'I can't do it.' This emotional attitude persists as long as the underlying cause is not addressed. If the situation continues, the emotion becomes stronger, taking over more and more of the brain's capacity for dealing with information (thinking), resulting in less capacity being available for solving the intellectual task, which further diminishes the capacity to find a solution, which then reinforces and reconfirms the student's sense of inability. This particular scenario is very common and extreme in pupils with the (rare) disorder of Prader-Willi syndrome. It is often the extremes that emphasize the existence of the same problem, at lower levels, in many other people.

If students experience this situation frequently, then they will gradually withdraw from more and more schoolwork, refusing to take the risks that are necessary for learning to occur.

An extremely intelligent and academically successful former student explained to me his way of dealing with perceived risks. He explained that his strategy dealt with hearing the words 'Never mind, you did your best'... a phrase that he hated to hear. He said that he tried to eliminate the possibility of hearing those words by appraising any task he was about to meet. If he felt he could succeed, then he would start the task. If he felt that the task would result in failure the he would not start the task. No task, no failure, no 'Never mind'...

'Never mind, you did your best' is well intentioned, but does not raise or even protect self-esteem. The avoidance, no risk reaction may well be one of the reasons behind classroom behaviours 1, 2 and 15 from the CBL.

The occurrence of risk avoidance can be influenced by the way lessons are structured. For example, Johnson *et al.* (1984) describe how lessons can be structured competitively where students work against each other. It is implicit in this type of structure that not all students will attain success, or, at least, will not perceive that they succeed. If such a structure is not closely managed, there is the chance that some students succeed only if other students fail.

CHAPTER 15

TRANSACTIONAL ANALYSIS

One of the key issues highlighted by the CBL is the issue of communication, effective communication. The nine behaviours (taken from the CBL) listed below may be a consequence for a child who has not learned to respond appropriately to the verbal and non-verbal communication of his peers.

8.   Accepting critism from teacher

9.   Accepting criticism from peers

12.   Interferes with other students' work

14.   Makes inappropriate comments in class

21.   Unable to work on group tasks

24.   Misinterprets instructions

25.   Misinterprets social communication

31.   Unable to form friendships

32.   Limited participation in social activities

One of the interesting and pragmatic approaches to communication is Transactional Analysis. Although Transactional Analysis dates back to the 1960s, it still has relevance today.

It is not my intention to provide a detailed explanation of Transactional Analysis in this book (for more detail, see e.g. Barrow, Bradshaw and Newton 2001; Berne 1975; Harris 1969). As with the other key concepts covered in the second part of this book, I simply want to illustrate why I think it is one of the valuable concepts to have 'on call' when making decisions about any interactions with students with special needs. These concepts develop the skills for those occasions when the 'What to do on Monday' strategies do not deal with a particular situation.

Like Kohlberg's theories on moral development (see Chapter 12), Transactional Analysis has been around a while and is not widely used at present (at least not overtly). However, it does provide pragmatic guidance and explanations for that complex subject, communication.

Communication is the key skill at the heart of managing classroom behaviours. The skill of good communication depends on many subskills and attitudes and thus goes far beyond the words used.

Students with special needs may not be good at communication, often as a consequence of their special needs. This puts three major obligations on teachers and other adults working with these students:

- The first obligation is to recognize and actively acknowledge that the student's special needs may impact on their communication skills, both verbal and non-verbal.

- The second obligation is to find ways of improving the student's communication skills.

- The third obligation is to find ways to make one's own skills more effective for the sake of effective and clear communication with the student.

While I deal with my choice of key concepts in separate chapters, there is no doubt that they interlink and sometimes overlap, for example, as explained on pp.90–92, Spence (1995) explains the role of communication in developing social skills and competence. These are sophisticated cognitive abilities that may challenge the skills of many students with special needs.

The outcomes from intervention to help communication may not always meet the expectations of the teacher.

There was a student with Asperger characteristics at my school. As he came in to breakfast, where I would serve the coffee or tea each day, he would leave the serving counter with the words, 'Have a nice day, Sir'. After a few weeks of this same phrase, I suggested that he could slip in some variations, such as, 'Have a great day' or 'Have a fascinating day' or 'Have a happy day'. He would say, 'OK. Have a great day' as he left, but I still got 'Have a nice day' the next day. He had a social skill, but was unable to develop this particular communication towards flexibility and social competence.

Transactional Analysis (TA) is one way to help us understand and improve our communication skills (as teachers and as adults). I find the underlying principles reassuringly sensible and astute. TA looks at both of the people involved in the communication and analyses what they say, the ego-state the speaker is in when he or she speaks and the ego-state of the recipient (colloquially, 'where they are coming from'). TA provides a structure for understanding and improving communication.

Transactions, communications between two people, can be complementary or crossed. So, each time we communicate we enter into a transaction. If the transactions are complementary they can go on forever. If the transactions are crossed the result will be a breakdown in communication. Transactional

Analysis is about developing mutual empathy in communications and thus in the outcomes of those communications. Children with special needs are often more in need of empathic communication if they are to avoid breakdowns in their communications with others. TA helps to remind us that we have to consider both and the listener and the speaker in any communication.

Although TA deals with all types of social communications, it is particularly relevant when it is used to deal with the included child. It can help to reduce the chances of conflict arising from misunderstandings. The benefits of using Transactional Analysis techniques include the following:

- Students can be helped to initiate and maintain a mutually empathetic conversation (and thus enhance social interactions).

- Students and adults can understand why they say what they say in a particular way and then helped to anticipate the effect it will have on the communication process.

- Students and adults should be able to predict (more accurately) how their communication may be received by the other person.

- Students and adults learn to understand that what they say and how they say it either makes a conversation continue smoothly or become confrontational.

- Students can be helped to build positive relationships based on mutual respect, thus improving their behaviour.

In the 1970s Transactional Analysis became known colloquially as the 'I'm OK, you're OK' theory of communication. 'I'm OK, you're OK' could be rephrased as, 'I feel calm and content with myself and I respect and accept you.'

That message alone can boost self-esteem and confidence for a student with special needs. It will help to build a positive relationship between student and teacher. The student needs to understand and be aware that this is the underlying message behind every communication. Good communication skills are essential when dealing with students with special needs because the teacher or adult bears even more responsibility for the success of their communications than they would with the student without those special needs. Also, each communication can be so much more than just the instruction or the explanation. Successful communication builds relationships and trust.

EGO STATES

A key part of the Transactional Analysis theory is that we, as people, can take on, at any time, one of three ego states, which are, basically, the way we feel when we speak. The ego state we adopt will influence the way we communicate and the outcome of the communication.

The ego state of the person with whom we are communicating will also affect the communication. The three ego states are labelled as 'Parent', 'Adult' and 'Child'.

When a person is in the *Parent ego state*, she or he acts, feels, talks and thinks just as a parent would with a child, most likely based on her or his own experiences of her or his parents when she or he was young. The Parent ego state is about how we take responsibility for ourselves and for others. We can be a *Controlling Parent* or a *Nurturing Parent*. Both can be either positive or negative in their effect on the communication, because the communication is a transaction, an interaction between two people.

The Parent ego state has two main functions. It enables an individual to act as a parent of actual children, an important characteristic for society. It also makes many responses automatic: 'We do it that way, because that's the way we always do it', which can save a lot of time and energy for more important decisions. Of course, we have to select those occasions when this is the appropriate response and not make it the dominant response.

The Parent ego state consists of all the behaviours, thoughts and feelings we learned, absorbed and copied from the 'grown-ups' around us when we were young. There are implications here about the influence of role models in our society!

In the *Adult ego state* a person acts objectively, and is calculating and logical. Feelings are not involved. The Adult ego state is about making objective appraisals of reality, about making sense of what is going on around us. The Adult is necessary for survival, for example it decides if it is safe to overtake the car in front. The Adult is pragmatic and sensible (or somewhat like Mr Spock in *Star Trek*).

In the *Child ego state*, a person behaves in a childlike way (which is distinct from a childish way). Berne (1975, p.12) rated the Child ego state as the most valuable part of personality. The Child ego state represents ego states that were part of early childhood but are still active. The Child ego state can manifest as an *Adapted Child* or a *Natural Child*. Like the Parent ego state, these can be either positive or negative depending on the transaction. The Adapted Child will modify his or her behaviour under parental influence. The Natural Child is about spontaneous expression. Spontaneous expression can be creative or rebellious.

There is an obvious link here to body language (Wainwright 2003). People's body postures and expressions will usually give clues as to their ego state. For example, it would be difficult to stand with hands on hips, elbows bent (akimbo) and not be in a controlling parent state.

We can move quickly, or slowly, between ego states. As an example of this movement between ego states, think of driving a car. The Nurturing Parent stops to let a car into the queue of traffic. The Rebellious child speeds down the motorway at 90 mph. The Adult drives at 30mph through the speed limit because there are lots of pedestrians around and because the speed signs display 30.

The subcategories of the Parent and the Child ego states are summarized in Table 15.1. The subcategories can be positive and beneficial, or negative and detrimental.

Table 15.1 The subcategories of the Parent and Child ego states		
Controlling: Critical (negative) or Structuring (positive)	**Parent**	**Nurturing/Care:** Marshmallowy (negative) or Nurturing (positive)
	Adult	
Adapted: Cooperative (positive) or Compliant or Rebellious (negative)	**Child**	**Natural:** Spontaneous (positive) or Immature (negative)

A fuller picture of ego states is given in Table 15.2 courtesy of Barrow *et al.* (2001). There are cultural and evolutionary (in the sense that our societies are evolving) influences on these ego states. For example, the Parent, as illustrated by an authority figure such as a teacher, does not automatically command the instant respect it did some years ago (and even then not always if we are honest in our recollections of our own schooldays).

Table 15.2 Characteristics of modes

Mode	Attitude	Words	Posture, etc.	Example
Critical	Fault finding, adversarial, expect obedience, punitive, know best, threats, warning	'have to' 'should' 'must' 'never'	Standing over, wag finger, hands on hips, condescending, frowning	'Get out of my classroom – you never do as you're told – and don't bother coming back until you can behave.'
Structuring	Firm, inspiring, empowering, set limits, show expectations, give security, keep boundaries	'will' 'expect' (clear)	Controlled, solid, boundaried, focused, decisive	'Billy, you know the rule about talking when I'm talking, please listen so you will know what to do.'
Marshmallowy	Fussing, over-protective, smothering, over-indulgent, sugary, too close	'let me' 'poor thing' 'I'll help you'	Soothing, touching, leaning over someone	'Don't worry if you can't do it, Billy, I know you're having a bad time at home.'
Nurturing	Encouraging, empathetic, accepting, appreciative, understanding, available	'like' 'care' 'well done' 'do you want my help'	Open posture, smiling, concerned/ comforting	'Billy, I know it's difficult to concentrate. Come on, I'll help you to get started.'
Adult	Aware, objective, logical, practical, alert, thoughtful, receptive	'how' (questions, discussion)	Relaxed, interested, observant, eye contact	'OK, Billy, the rest of us are trying to get on with the work. Do you want to carry on here and finish it, or carry on at break time with me?'

Table 15.2 Characteristics of modes (*cont.*)

Mode	Attitude	Words	Posture, etc.	Example
Cooperative	Friendly, considerate, assertive, diplomatic, respectful, confident	'please' 'thanks' 'help' (asking, listening)	Attentive, restrained, polite, willing, sharing	'What is it you need help with, Billy? Well done for putting your hand up.'
Compliant or Rebellious	Conforming, anxious, pleasing, whiny, withdrawn/ obstinate, rebellious, defiant, aggresive	'can't' 'won't' 'try' 'wish'	Collased, closed, pouting, willing, sharing	'No, you can't go to the toilet! I'm fed up with you messing about in my class.'
Spontaneous	Playful, creative, energetic, vital, expressive, motivated, curious	'wow' 'great' 'fun' 'want'	Loose, unselfconscious, enthusiastic, head on on side, happy	'Right, come on you lot. Let's have a race. Whoever gets the answer to question two first can choose what we do forthe last five minutes.'
Immature	Irresponsible, selfish, careless, inconsiderate, thoughtless	'won't' 'me' 'my' 'no'	Out of control, inappropriate, emotional, over loud	'Well, let them wait in the cold. i've got my coffee to finish.'

Source: courtesy of Barrow et al. (2001)

TRANSACTIONAL ANALYSIS: THE ANALYSIS OF TRANSACTIONS

Transactional Analysis, not surprisingly, considers and analyses communication in terms of transactions. In part, this involves considering the ego state – Parent, Adult or Child – of those involved on either side of the transaction. These ego states are not necessarily permanent within the individual or within a conversation, but may change as the transactions change.

A transaction as stimulus and response

Since Transactional Analysis is about two people and each person can be in one of the three ego-states, then there are 81 possible combinations of transactions, of stimulus and response. Of these 81, Berne classifies nine as 'complementary' and considers that only four of the 'crossed' transactions occur frequently in everyday life (Berne 1975, p.14).

When transactions are complementary, conversations can carry on indefinitely. When transactions are crossed, communication breaks down. It may well be that being aware of the 'breakdown' transactions will make handling pupils with special needs less prone to conflict.

Some examples of transactions

- Adult–Adult: the Adult decides that it is safe to overtake. The other Adult in the car ahead pulls over towards the side of the road to allow the overtaking to be safer.

- Child–Parent: the Child says, 'I have a sore throat' and the Nurturing Parent gives her a spoonful of medicine, accompanied by some comforting words.

- Parent–Parent: the Parent says, 'That Michelle couldn't boil an egg.' The responsive Parent says, 'And she never seems to iron any of her clothes properly.'

- Parent–Child and Child–Child: playing a board game together.

All these transactions are complementary, that is the response is appropriate and expected from the nature of the stimulus. Transactions that are complementary result in communication that continues smoothly. The nature of transactions is irrelevant as long as they are complementary.

A complementary transaction occurs if the stimulus transaction and the response transaction do not cross as in the examples shown in Figures 15.1 and 15.2. In the diagrams, P=Parent, A=Adult and C=Child.

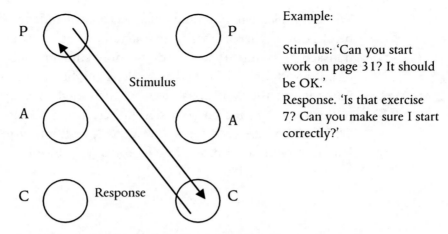

Example:

Stimulus: 'Can you start work on page 31? It should be OK.'
Response. 'Is that exercise 7? Can you make sure I start correctly?'

Figure 15.1 A complementary PC–CP transaction

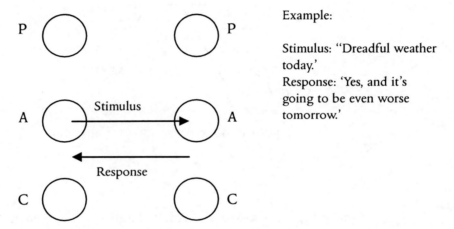

Example:

Stimulus: ''Dreadful weather today.'
Response: 'Yes, and it's going to be even worse tomorrow.'

Figure 15.2 A complementary AA–AA transaction

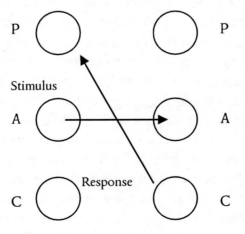

Figure 15.3 A crossed AA–CP transaction

While complementary transactions can carry on indefinitely, communication breaks down when a crossed transaction occurs. The most common crossed transaction is the Type I, Adult–Adult stimulus and the Child–Parent response (Figure 15.3). For example, I might ask my secretary, 'Do you know where the Comenius file is?' which might generate an Adult–Adult response of 'Yes, it's on your desk' (there could be just a hint of Parent–Child in the tone used for that response!) or it might generate the Child–Parent response of 'I didn't lose it. You always blame me for losing things.'

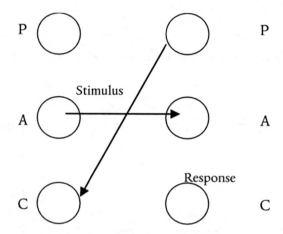

Figure 15.4 A crossed AA–PC transaction

In a Type II crossed the Adult–Adult stimulus generates a Parent–Child response, as in 'Do you know where the Comenius file is?' which receives the response of 'Find it yourself. It's time you learned to find your own files.'

At a potentially contentious interview with the deputy headteacher of a mainstream school where a 15-year-old girl was experiencing inclusion, or exclusion at this particular time, the father, sitting some way away from the deputy, was explaining, with his customary use of supplementary non-verbal communication via lots of hand movements, in this case a waist-level downward-moving counting finger, a list of points to be discussed, when the deputy leaned forward in his chair and said, 'We don't use batons here.' It could be interpreted as an Adult–Adult stimulus, in that a fact was stated. Or it could be a Parent–Child stimulus in that it was instructing the Rebellious Child. Just how that conversation continued would depend entirely on the response. The stimulus abandoned any control of the conversation. If the response was something along the lines of, 'I see you have had some basic training in communication skills. Isn't it time you took the advanced course', then that could be taken as an Adult–Adult response. But the true, hidden meaning of that response was Parent–Child, along the lines of 'I think you know very little about communication skills and your attitude could be construed as condescending.' This is an example of what Berne (1975) calls a Duplex Transaction (Adult–Adult) where there is an underlying psychological or covert level to the transaction. (The response used by the parent was to push both hands in his jacket pockets and say, 'Sorry, I always use my hands when I talk. Will this make you feel more comfortable?' The deputy did not pick up the covert meaning of this Adult–Adult (less obviously) Duplex Transaction.) The conversation continued.

In this next example, where, inevitably, the student or the teacher could control the outcome of the communication, the teacher is asking a student to begin independent study. The ego states are identified for each communication and therefore for each transaction.

T: Come on then Joe. Get out your book so you can start on your geography revision. P–C

S: I haven't got it. C (Rebellious)–P

T: Where is it? P–C

S: It's in room 5. C–P

T: Why didn't you get it during break? P (Critical)–C

S: I'm not doing it then, that's my own time! C (Rebellious)–P

T: Well you can't go now because another lesson has started in that room. P (Critical)–C

S: Well it'll be your fault if I fail my exam then! C (Rebellious)–P

If Joe had had enough social skills to anticipate the outcome of that sequence of transactions, he would have realized that the teacher would be disappointed at best and cross at worst with his forgetfulness and would have used a different strategy:

T: Come on then, Joe. Get out your book so you can start on your geography revision. P–C

S: Oh! I'm sorry I forgot to get it during break. I'll run over and see if the teacher in the room will let me pick it up it now! C (Compliant)–P

T: OK, Joe. Don't be long and try to remember next time! P (Nurturing)–C

It could be argued that the outcome of this second series of transactions was controlled by the pupil when he showed good communication skills.

Usually it is the teacher who has more chances to control communications. In terms of managing transactions in the classroom, the teacher usually has the power to keep transactions complementary and not let them become crossed (unless she or he chooses otherwise). This requires the teacher to engage in constant Transactional Analysis, or anticipate a transaction becoming crossed and take evasive action with his or her next transaction, or, if the crossed transaction still takes place, recognize it and make sure that the next response is not crossed too, or the communication will really break down.

I'M OK, YOU'RE OK

Berne's work has been colloquially summed up as 'I'm OK. You're OK.' which, in a transaction, infers how we feel about ourselves and how we feel about the recipient. In fact there are four combinations of OK and not OK:

- I'm OK. You're not OK.
- I'm not OK. You're OK.
- I'm not OK. You're not OK.
- I'm OK. You're OK.

Students who have low self-esteem may feel 'I'm not OK' most of the time and this will have a strong influence on all their transactions. The more the teacher can take the student towards 'I'm OK', the more productive transactions will be. There is a strong link to self-esteem and self-concept here.

'I'm OK. You're OK.' is the best combination, because it implies respect for self and for others, and this will be confirmed or contradicted by the transaction we give and receive. Stroking (see section on 'Praise and strokes') from an 'I'm OK. You're OK.' attitude is always positive, even if the message being given is not welcome. This stroking is based on respect and care and a belief that the other person can do something differently.

It matters where criticism comes from, that is who makes the criticism. Candidates in the reality TV show *The Apprentice* are under no illusion that they will be criticized by Sir Alan Sugar and they have to acquiesce, even if it is not from an 'I'm OK. You're OK.' position.

PRAISE AND STROKES

Berne states that we all have recognition-hunger and consequently we all need strokes to sustain us (Berne 1975, p.21). A stroke can be a look, a touch, a smile or a comment. Some students (and adults) need many strokes, but others need only a few.

The word 'stroke' is used in Transactional Analysis to denote any act implying recognition of another's presence. A stroke may be viewed as the fundamental unit of social action. An autistic child may lack the ability to provide this fundamental unit of social interaction.

Stroke theory is partly about positive and negative reinforcements, but not surprisingly, it is not that simple. Once again we have to consider the individual. Some special needs pupils come to a lesson (or a new school) with a history of mostly negative experiences. They may well not be ready for too many (in their perception) positive strokes. Their sense of balance of positive and negative may not be ready for an imbalance of positive strokes and they may respond with negatives. The only way a teacher can find out the stroke needs of a student is by trial and error! Even then, this may well not be a stable parameter. Children with special needs are often 'labile' (unpredictable).

Stroke theory links to attributional theory (see Chapter 16) in that it will be the strokes that modify an attribution, so it will be important that the strokes given to challenge an attribution are acceptable to the pupil.

As was said above, good and bad influences and strokes are not always as simple as they may seem. For example, praising *ability* can make pupils worry more about failing in the future and thus take fewer risks, whereas praising *effort* encourages more effort, persistence and resilience. This is a partial explanation as to why some educators advise 'Praise the work, not the child.'

Some of the pupils who are just not ready for strokes will, if praised for good behaviour one day, balance out their perception of reality by behaving badly the next day. It may be that they are protecting the image they have created with their peers. Maintaining self-concept can be a self-fulfilling prophecy, of course.

DISCOUNTS

The 'discount' aspect of TA is also closely linked to attributional theory. Discounting can be an internal process by which people distort reality. Discounts belittle an offered stroke, for example, 'That was a great essay you wrote.' 'Not really, I had such a lot of help from my tutor.'

Discounts can also be given, for example, instead of the nurturing 'You made a small basic fact error with that sum', a teacher could use the critical, 'You really don't get this work, do you!' The latter, critical communication makes a temporary and specific situation seem personal, permanent and pervasive (see Chapter 16 on attributional style).

INTERACTIONS OF TA WITH OTHER CONSTRUCTS

The constructs (psychological theories) covered in this book not only interact with each other, but also interact with many other constructs not covered by a seperate and specific chapter in this book. For example, Transactional Analysis interacts with directive and responsive expressions.

DIRECTIVE AND RESPONSIVE EXPRESSIONS

What a teacher actually says and how she or he says it may have different implications for different pupils. There is a difference between *directive* and *responsive* expressions. Not all students may pick up on the differences.

When a teacher sets a task and expects the pupil to do this task in accordance with the teacher's conditions, the teacher is *directive* in her or his interaction with the pupil. This applies to standard instructive and controlling expressions like:

- John, pay attention!
- Mary, look again!
- No, you should do it like this!
- Go on!
- You have to do page 24 first.
- You have to do six more problems.

A teacher's verbal expressions are mainly *responsive*, when she or he enables the pupil to answer questions, assess choices and form an opinion of the task. Examples are:

- John, what strikes you about this story?
- Mary, are you looking at the right picture?
- Do you think you might be able to do this problem by a different method?
- Do you think you could do page 24?
- Could you do these two problems in the five minutes we have left?

The most striking linguistic difference between directive and responsive expressions is that the former uses the imperative, whereas the latter mostly uses the interrogative. The pupil's as well as the teacher's perspectives of the task are central in responsive expressions. However, not all expressions are that easily categorized. It is often a matter of more or less. In a classroom situation it may be possible to initiate a gradual change from directive towards responsive expressions, creating a smooth transition from directive towards responsive. This may require the teacher to try systematically to express himself more responsively in conversations with pupils.

In Transactional Analysis theory this is equivalent to the difference between the 'controlling' and the 'nurturing' parent. Sometimes 'controlling' is appropriate in that it deals swiftly with a situation, as in, 'Start on page four, question six'.

Again, it is worth remembering that interventions cannot transform every deficit or at the other extreme, assume that a student will just 'grow out of it' without interventions.

At a meeting of former students I was standing as part of a circle with these students when another former student came into the middle of the circle and moved to face me, too close by normal social standards and with his back to most of the group, and proceeded to engage me in a one-to-one conversation, thus cutting out the rest of his group. Three years after leaving school, that particular social skill deficit was even more apparent. We didn't always succeed in all our goals!

CHAPTER 16

ATTRIBUTIONAL STYLE

I learned about attributional style and Dr Martin Seligman (see Seligman 2006) in the late 1990s from a psychologist who was working for a large UK insurance company. He told me that he was doing some interesting work with cold-call telephone operatives and with people who had been unemployed for a long time. Both these groups received a lot of negative feedback in their daily lives. In the case of the cold-call operatives, the consequence was that they became demotivated and did not stay long with the company. For the long-term unemployed people, each failed interview made it harder to raise the motivation to apply again for another job.

An Australian psychiatrist, working in the UK, Dr J. Proudfoot applied explanatory style theory (and intervention) with success to the long-term unemployed. The characteristics of this unemployed group are very similar to those of many special needs pupils. They have

- reduced self-esteem
- reduced self-efficacy
- low expectations of success
- low motivation to seek work
- little or no self-belief.

ATTRIBUTIONAL STYLE AND SPECIAL NEEDS

It seemed to me that my dyslexic pupils had also experienced that same overwhelming avalanche of negative feedback. What was exciting for me was that the psychologist had introduced me to attributional style as a tool to address the learned helplessness of many of my students and to a theory that offered much more than 'raising self-esteem', a phrase that featured in many Statements of Special Educational Needs that came with my students.

What also encouraged me to follow up on this construct was that it also helped to build resilience in a population that was often emotionally fragile.

I needed to find more ways to encourage an ethos of risk taking when in learning situations for my special needs students.

My new awareness of attributional style theory coincided with an encounter that cast doubt on the efficacy of 'raising self-esteem'. An habitually critical inspector from a funding authority who had visited the school for many years told me at the end of one of his visits: 'Your problem is, Steve, that you give your students far too much self-esteem' (see also p.100). My initial reactions were astonishment and surprise that this might be a compliment or that it might also be a ridiculous statement. As I thought about the comment over the next few days, I began to see some validity in the comment. Some of our Year 11 (16-year-old) students were a little too confident at times, for example, over the need to revise for end-of-year examinations. I could see the risks in raising self-esteem as well as the benefits. As I looked more closely into attributional style, I became convinced that this was a construct that had far more to offer to my students than 'raising self-esteem'.

The outcomes of integrating the theories of attributional style into my school were evaluated by Burden (2005) in his book *Dyslexia and Self-Concept*.

> Interestingly the outcomes of this investigation did not turn out quite as expected because, basically, the school proved to be outstanding in what it set out to do, i.e. to turn dyslexic 'losers' into academic and sporting 'winners'. What our interviews showed, in contrast to most previous research studies was that, with the right kind of educational provision, people with dyslexia do not necessarily have to suffer from lifelong feelings of learned helplessness or depression, but can develop strong feelings of self-efficacy and internal locus of control which can make a powerful contribution towards academic success at 16. (Burden 2005, p.79)

EXPLAINING TO OURSELVES WHY THINGS HAPPEN TO US

Attributional style acknowledges that there is a strong tendency for people to seek out reasons as to why things, especially things that concern themselves, happen. One aspect of this tendency is the way in which we attribute causes to events that happen in our lives, thus developing our 'attributional style'. We naturally look for causes or attributions for the behaviour of ourselves and of others and we also look for causal links between our own actions and their effects.

Seligman (2006) believes we all have a predominant 'explanatory style'. He labels the two explanatory styles as 'negative and pessimist' and 'positive and optimist'.

When we encounter adversity, we react by thinking about it. Our thoughts become beliefs and the beliefs become habitual and we become optimists or pessimists, positive or negative.

One aspect of attribution is our sense of whether the control of events is from within – an internal locus of control, or from external factors – an external locus of control. Many special needs children experience an extreme form of an external locus of control, exacerbated by a constant barrage of negative feedback that results in a negative, apathetic and withdrawn approach to situations. In other words they feel as though they have no control over events in their lives, especially events related to school.

SUCCESS AND FAILURE

Attributional style can explain why some students succeed and others fail. For example, positive attributional style is strongly associated with high performance and success. Weiner (1985), another worker in this field, suggests three main dimensions for the causes of success and failure:

- *Stability* is about whether the cause (or causes) changes or not. Ability and intelligence are usually perceived as stable causes, whereas effort can change. A variable attribution is easier to influence than a stable attribution.

- *Internal or external* is about whether the cause comes from within the individual or from outside. Internal causes include ability and effort. External causes include the characteristics of the task, for example 'Fractions are just too hard to understand!'

- *Controllability* is about whether the result can or cannot be affected by the person making more effort. Traits such as laziness are under voluntary control. Physical coordination as in many cases of dyspraxia is not.

Effort plays a key role in all three dimensions. For example, we can apply these dimensions to how a pupil might explain his success in maths:

internal	internal	external	external
stable	**variable**	**stable**	**variable**
'I understand this type of maths problems really well.'	'I worked hard at that topic.'	'That was an easy topic.'	'I was lucky. The right questions came up in the test.'

Or to explain his failure at reading:

internal	internal	external	external
stable	**variable**	**stable**	**variable**
'I'm always very nervous when it's my turn to read.'	'I didn't know some of the difficult words.'	'Those stories are rubbish!'	'It was just my bad luck that they chose a book about something I hate.'

PERMANENCE, PERSONALIZATION AND PERVASIVE

Seligman (2006) also describes three dimensions of explanatory style. His descriptions are very similar to Weiner, but his labels are different.

- *Permanence:* people who give up easily believe that the bad events that happen to them are permanent. This results in feeling helpless and that you are unable to influence events. People who resist becoming 'helpless' believe the causes of bad events are temporary. For example:

    Permanent (and pessimistic): 'I won't ever be able to write essays.'

    Temporary (and optimistic): 'I'm having difficulty with the history essay our teacher set this week.'

- *Personalization:* when a bad event happens we can blame ourselves (internalize) or other people or circumstances (externalize). People who consistently blame themselves for bad events have low self-esteem and each new self-blame will push that self-esteem to even lower levels. People who blame external factors do not lose self-esteem when a bad event occurs. For example:

    Internal (low self-esteem): 'I'm too stupid to understand physics.'

    External (high self-esteem): 'My teacher doesn't explain things well.'

- *Pervasive:* when a bad event happens to a person he can believe that 'Nothing ever goes right for me' (universal). Or he can believe that the bad event was a one-off and that it has no influence on future events (specific). For example:

    Universal (pessimistic): 'I can't draw animals, I can't draw anything.'

> **Specific (optimistic): 'I am not very good at drawing horses, but I am good at drawing people.'**

I used attributional style in my school more as an underlying, integrated philosophy rather than as a ready-made intervention programme like, for example, many of the social skills programmes. However, Seligman's (2006) book on attributional style *Learned Optimism* does include questionnaires and specific examples of intervention. As with many of the social skills programmes, attributional style is based on cognitive behaviour therapy, teaching people to analyse a situation and then, in Seligman's model, to view it with 'learned optimism'. Attributional style provides a way of channelling a person's thinking so that he or she views situations and events from a positive, optimistic perspective.

OPTIMISM AND PESSIMISM

Being an optimist or being a pessimist has a stong influence on how you perceive events and how you approach problems, whether big or small. These two conditions are important in Seligman's theories and on how people achieve success.

> **The problem with being a pessimist is that you are permanently miserable, and the problem with being an optimist is that you're often disappointed. It's best to be somewhere in between. (Desmond Morris, author of *The Human Zoo*)**

> **The advantage of being an optimist is that you are happier than the pessimist before the bad event happens. (A very loose quote from a long past episode of the television drama serial, *Grange Hill*)**

Some random observations on optimism and pessimism

'Pessimists minimize risk.' (Learning involves risk and learning for pupils with special needs generally involves more risk.) ADHD pupils tend to take risks and be optimists. Other special needs students are much less likely to take risks when learning. In the USA pessimism is called constructive negativity.

David Dunning of Cornell University, who studies optimism and pessimism, suggests that high levels of confidence are linked with high levels of incompetence (Dunning, Heath and Suls 2004).

Seligman (1998) believes there are numerous significant benefits to being optimistic while acknowledging that there are some times when pessimism is preferable.

SUCCESS

Seligman specifies three characteristics that determine success:

- aptitude, the ability to do a task

- motivation, the drive to do a task

- optimism, the belief that success will result from ability and effort.

A study I did some years ago (Chinn 1996) gave me an unexpected example of the role of motivation in academic achievement. I looked at the relationship between maths grades achieved by dyslexic students and their scores on the subtests of the Wechsler Intelligence Test, thinking that the scores might be the main predictors of achievement. However, for the students within the average IQ band (90-110) the biggest factor in their success was their motivation and attitude. While these characteristics were not measured with a psychometric test, the subjects were all students at my school and I had a good subjective evaluation of these characteristics. I know, from my experience of working in the special needs field, that motivation is an essential component of success in any subject for such pupils. I also know that optimism can be a powerful factor in their success.

In a survey of the attributional style of pupils at my secondary school for dyslexic students, the students with comorbid (co-occurring) ADHD were the most optimistic. They just kept bouncing back! The same survey identified the students with a severe pessimistic attributional style. Fortunately our pastoral care system had already flagged up these students, but it did convince me of the efficacy of the attributional style concept and Seligman's Children's Attributional Style Questionnaire (Seligman 2006, p.116), even though it is based on US culture and language.

APTITUDE, MOTIVATION AND OPTIMISM

Special needs can impact on any of Seligman's three characteristics of aptitude, motivation and optimism. The learning difficulties of a student can have a direct effect on the perception by others of their aptitude, for example often depressing some teachers' judgements of their true potential. This, in turn, affects the student's own self-perceptions causing failures to be seen as personal. Also, if effort does not result in adequate, acceptable and appropriate rewards, internally or from external sources, then students may feel that events are permanent and pervasive.

Motivation can be hugely affected by the way students attribute their failures and successes. Unlike self-esteem, which is a limited concept, attribution can be more broadly influential on a student's motivation and resilience. In order to change attributional style to a more positive dimension, a student's attributions need to be challenged almost constantly (see p. 127).

It is not surprising that special needs children can be pessimistic. Changing their pessimism to optimism is not going to happen as a result of once-a-month counselling sessions. Intervention for addressing negative attributions should permeate the ethos of the school, with especial targeting of every special needs child.

Adults and children can be assessed for their attributional style by using Seligman's questionnaires (Seligman 2006, pp.33 and 116). Those who attribute their failures to internal, stable and global factors and their successes to external, temporary and specific causes are vulnerable to poor levels of persistence, impaired performance and depression. We have to be careful that special needs students do not enter a downward spiral to depression and withdrawal.

LISTENING TO PUPILS

While Seligman has devised a diagnostic Children's Attributional Style Questionnaire, substantial information can be collected from informal observations over a period of time and in different settings, which in some ways will make the subsequent deductions more reliable than those from a one-off questionnaire. Listening to pupils gives clues as to their attributions for explaining failure.

Attributions of pupils
Internal and stable

'I'm too stupid to understand this.'

'I just can't concentrate, ever.'

These statements suggest that the pupil does not feel in control of any challenge or task. This situation will not respond to a 'quick fix' intervention.

Internal and variable

'I didn't have time to read the notes properly.'

'I had a lot of other things on my mind that day.'

The student believes that the causes of failure are temporary and specific and can be addressed immediately.

External and stable

'That teacher will never be able to teach me physics.'

'My textbook is useless.'

The student blames external and permanent factors for his failure. This will be another long-term challenge for his teachers!

External and variable

'The wrong questions came up on the exam paper.'

'The noise outside the classroom today stopped me from concentrating.'

The student blames an external dimension. Consequently, things may be better next time and he will probably try again. This attribution helps build resilience.

Attributions of teachers

It is worth noting that the attributions of teachers are as important as the attributions of their pupils. After all, both are involved in the learning process. Four combinations of dimensions are given below to illustrate how a teacher may explain the causes of a bad lesson.

Internal and stable

'Science is not my specialist subject.'

'I could never do maths myself.'

The teacher's attribution focuses on his lack of skill in the subject. It is his lack of skill for that subject that will not change.

Internal and variable

'I had no time to prepare that lesson.'

'I was so tired.'

The cause is lack of effort. The teacher can make more effort next time.

External and stable

> **'My group is too big.'**
>
> **'It's such a challenging group.'**
>
> **'It's this government. What do they know about education?'**

The factors are beyond the teacher's control and are perceived as permanent.

External and variable

> **'It was just one of those lessons.'**
>
> **'Class 9Z were just having a bad day.'**

Failure is attributed to a one-off bad day and was not therefore the teacher's fault!

BEING DEPRESSED

It is so sad to see children who are depressed, yet there seem to be more and more children who suffer from depression. Depression is a manifestation of helplessness. The children feel that they have no control whatsoever over the events in their lives. Depressed children are very pessimistic. However, being pessimistic and even being depressed have some positive consequences. Most depressed people may have negative thought patterns, but they can be more realistic than optimists or non-depressed people. For example, depressed people

- will have equal memories of positive and negative experiences
- accept responsibility for failures as well as successes
- have realistic views of the future
- will not exaggerate how competent or well liked they are.

However, there are some negative consequences. Depressed behaviour can influence the way others react to you, so depressed behaviour can trigger aggression and anxiety in others. Depressed pupils can become socially isolated.

Depression can be a vicious cycle, a self-fulfilling prophesy of inability. A negative learning experience leads to self-blame, which leads to a depressed mood, which leads to other people reacting negatively towards you, which leads to more negative experiences, and so on. Alternatively, a negative social experience leads to self-blame and negative feelings about others, which leads to negative conversations and interactions with other people, which leads to negative reactions from other people, which leads to more negative social experiences, and so on.

There are many reasons for including social skills training in the curriculum for pupils with special needs, but it is worth noting that researchers in the UK have suggested that a depressed attributional style may act as a barrier which hinders the ability to generalize and internalize traditional behaviour modification methods. In other words attributional style has to be addressed first.

BEING HAPPY

It seems that attributional style is becoming more widely known in the UK. However, certain sections of the press have focused on 'happiness lessons'. This narrow focus trivializes the enormous benefits that can accrue from a sensible integration of attributional style into a school's ethos.

It is said that happiness is not dependent on age or gender, but can vary from country to country. For example the Costa Ricans self-rate their happiness higher than the Portuguese do (Veenhoven 2006). Happiness does not depend on wealth (though I would like to conduct well-funded, luxury research study on this).

Four characteristics have been related to happiness (Myers 1993). Happy people

- are comfortable with themselves and have high self-esteem
- feel in control of their lives
- have optimism and hope
- are extrovert.

It is one of our obligations as educators working with pupils who have special needs to make their time in school as happy as possible, or at least minimize the miserable time. The first three of the characteristics above can be addressed for pupils with special needs by the interventions discussed in this book. It may be more challenging to try to make someone extrovert.

BEING SUCCESSFUL

To repeat Seligman's requirements for success from earlier in this chapter, there are three characteristics that determine success:

- aptitude
- motivation
- optimism.

Aptitude

Pupils with special needs may not present with behaviours that reflect their true aptitude. This may be due to a physical difficulty, for example, poor fine motor control that diminishes their ability to record their thoughts comprehensively, or it may be due to a specific cognitive problem such as an inability to spell words which results in the use of a reduced vocabulary. Judgements of their work may be based on their poor spelling rather than the content of the essay. It is important to give genuine praise for their work. It is equally important not to praise their intelligence as that may lead to emotional fragility when work is not as good.

Motivation

Motivation depends a lot on the acknowledgement and recognition of past successes. It also depends on the belief that the task will be completed successfully, or the student may choose not to start on a task if he predicts failure when first appraising the task. Unfortunately many pupils with Special Educational Needs and Disability (SEND) do not have a reservoir of past successes to sustain motivation. Hence another reason to give genuine praise whenever possible, while remaining aware of discounts and the internal balance for praise and criticism (see Chapter 15 on Transactional Analysis).

Optimism

Optimism is partly about believing the outcome will be successful or that a failure is only temporary and that another attempt is worthwhile because success will happen this time. Many ADHD students have this 'bounce back' optimism. Although a student may well be optimistic in general, the reality of school for many students with special needs is about pessimism. It is more realistic (in their perception) and self-protecting to believe they will fail.

Importance of self-belief

Pupils have to believe that the effort they make on a task will make a difference and that the efforts they have made will be acknowledged by adults. It is motivating if they see that effort has a positive affect on the way they themselves feel about the tasks. Sometimes it is hard for adults to appreciate how much effort has been given to what looks like a substandard response to a set task.

Quotes from Lance Armstrong, winner of the Tour de France seven times, survivor of testicular cancer that spread to his lungs and brain, illustrate Seligman's beliefs:

> When I was sick, I didn't want to die. When I race, I don't want to lose.

> [About drug-enhanced sport] People want to know that the guy who worked the hardest and fought the hardest and got the best coaches and the best team mates went out there and won fair and square.

> [About cancer] It is who I am and it is the reason I am what I am. I credit it with a lot of the success I have had because it encouraged me to fight and to go out and get success on a bike.

CHALLENGING NEGATIVE ATTRIBUTIONS AND ADVERSITY

Challenging negative attributions requires adults to listen to how the pupil explains the good and bad events that happen and then challenge the student's beliefs empathetically and constructively. Choosing the optimum time to discuss situations and events is often as critical as what is subsequently said.

The student should be talked through the situation and his or her beliefs using Seligman's (2006) five steps, which he labels as ABCDE:

- **A**dversity is the situation, be it a leaking tap or a bad homework.

- **B**elief is the way the adversity is interpreted. Beliefs are not to be confused with feelings.

- **C**onsequences can be feelings and what was done.

- **D**isputation (and Distraction) deals with a pessimistic reaction. The student learns to challenge his or her beliefs by considering evidence and by looking for alternative, more positive beliefs. Seligman explains how to argue with yourself by considering evidence, alternatives, implications and usefulness.

- **E**nergization is about implementing the outcome.

ABCDE is a cognitive therapy targeted to a goal of an optimistic explanatory style. As with any cognitive therapy, the student must understand the steps, the actions and the potential outcomes. As has been said before, this places a responsibility on the adult charged with the task to explain the processes clearly (but not in a patronizing way).

The process can be used to pre-empt negativity.

When the Head of Maths at my school taught simultaneous equations, she taught it over three sessions, separated by other work.

In the first session she tells the students, 'We are going to look at simultaneous equations. You will find this topic difficult first time because every group does, but stay with me. We will be looking at this again in a couple of weeks and then again in another two weeks and then you will understand it.' And, despite some good teaching, many of the group do find the topic difficult at first exposure. Some students might say, 'This is difficult, Miss.' And she would say, 'Yes. I told you that you would find it difficult this first time.'

Then, after a couple of weeks there is the second lesson on simultaneous equations. A student might say, 'This is better, but I still don't really get it.' And she would say, 'That's what I told you. Be patient. We have our third session left to come.'

At the end of the third lesson the pupils say, 'OK. I get this now.' She says, 'That's great.'

Attributional challenges work for teachers, too.

- *Adversity*: 'I spend a long time talking to a pupil about his bullying of other boys and helping him to understand that it is a harmful activity for the other boys and himself.' He is caught bullying the next day.

- *Belief*: 'I'm just not good at counselling. I didn't help at all. Everyone will know I have failed.'

- *Consequences*: 'I felt inadequate. I felt like giving up on the pupil.'

- *Disputation*: 'This boy has been a bully for a long time (evidence). It would be unrealistic to think I could change his behaviour after one session (evidence). I could try another counselling strategy (alternative). The incident was not as serious as usual (evidence). I should be patient and persevere with the boy (alternative).'

- *Energization*: 'I didn't feel such a failure. I feel that I will make a difference after a while. He's not all bad and can be changed.'

Challenging attributional style should be an essential ingredient of many interventions with pupils with special needs. Adults have to listen if they are to learn about the attributional style the student is demonstrating. The challenges to the existing style can be overt or covert, but the philosophy of building positive attributions should be ingrained into the ethos of the school.

APPRAISING ATTRIBUTIONAL STYLE

Attributional theory raises some questions (as do all interventions and good theories):

- Can all pupils accept and understand the implications of their (current) attributional style and see what problems might ensue?

- Can all pupils learn to modify their attributional style?

- Is it the 'right thing' for a school to do, or is too intrusive?

- Could all pupils, even those who do not present with problems or difficulties in school, benefit from understanding attributional style?

- Is it possible and/or desirable to target pupils with specific and other learning difficulties for identification and/or extra intervention?

- Should schools identify all 'at risk' pupils and then provide extra intervention?

- Can the necessary skills for intervention be developed in schools? And who should have these skills?

- What topics and which subjects create pessimistic attributions? (And which teachers?)

WHAT IS THE ATTRIBUTION?

It is possible to become very observant and perceptive in picking up clues about pupils' attributional styles. Here is a little practice. What attribution is being revealed in each of these examples?

> **'I failed my exam because I am hopeless at exams.'**

> **'I didn't do my homework because I had to go and see my Grandma.'**

> **'I can't do maths. No one in my family can do maths.'**

> **'We lost the soccer game because our best player was ill.'**

> **'The depressing thing is that I spend hours learning my spellings at night, but I still forget them next morning.'**

Examples of attribution in life

Many times we have been lost. When I am navigating, it is my fault. When my husband is navigating, it is the fault of the map. (Barbara Martin, Letter to , 6 March 2004)

Mum, chop me up and throw me in the dustbin. I'm useless. I can't do the things that other kids can do. (Former dyslexic pupil, aged five, who went on to get seven GCSEs, the national exams for 16-year-old students in the UK, three Bs, three Cs and a D in English)

Mr H had a stupid moustache and was always telling me I was useless and no good and would never get anywhere in history. (Edwards 1994, p.37)

I backed my car out of my drive and hit a bus. It was not my fault as the bus was five minutes early. (From an insurance claim)

REINFORCING OR CHALLENGING ATTRIBUTIONAL STYLE

Consider how a student's attributional style is supported, gently challenged or reinforced by these two scenarios. A pupil is set a maths task: a number of division problems, starting with $14 \div 2$. The teacher (T) is instructing the student (S) in Scenario 1.

Scenario 1

T: This is your task. Use the materials I have given you to help you to work out the answers.

S: (Looks questioningly at the teacher)

T: Weren't you listening again? I told the group, you have to do these 15 division questions. Tell me, what does $14 \div 2$ mean?

S: Er…er…

T: Come on. Look, you have to get 14 cubes.

S: (Picks up two cubes and looks apprehensively at the teacher)

T: No, that's wrong. Look. You have to have 14 cubes. There is a child (points at the left-hand side of the table). This child gets one cube. There is another child (points to the right-hand side of the table) and that child gets one cube. Now you go on dividing these cubes equally.

S: (Sets out the 14 cubes)

T: That's OK. Now, you do the other sums in the same way. Do you think you can manage that?

S: (Nods hesitatingly)

T: Do this row of questions using the cubes. When I come back, you should have finished those questions in the first row. Then you can start on the second row of questions, without the cubes. I am expecting you to do all the questions on this page.

The teacher walks away and the pupil starts to work on the division questions. When the teacher returns after five minutes, the student has only reached the third sum.

T: You have only reached the third sum! So, you have only done one sum yourself. You must work harder. Just take a good look at each sum and then do it. And be careful with those cubes, you are making a mess. Which question are you doing now? 21 ÷ 3.

S: Three divided by…

T: No, it's the other way around! Think!

S: (Looks startled by the teacher's tone of voice)

T: 21 divided by three children. Here is one child and here and here. One cube here and one cube there and so on. Pay attention! Concentrate! You can do it if you try!'

A little later the teacher returns.

T: This is so disappointing. You have only done five questions in all this time! Why is that?

S: (Shrugs)

T: Do you know why you have only done so little?

S: It's so hot in here.

T: Humph! Any excuse! … (Walks away, shrugging his shoulders)

This example shows that the teacher has overlooked the student's need for meaningful (and appropriate) instruction and his feelings of insecurity, which will only be increased by this approach to classroom management. The teacher is also giving a clear message as to his own expectation of the student… 'You are not up to this work.'

The teacher has not adapted to the student's level of knowledge. His expectation of the student's ability to do several questions quickly is not realistic. The student does not get the chance to express or explain his lack of knowledge, nor does he get the opportunity to express his doubt about the feasibility of the assignment for him. The teacher makes a cursory attempt to find out the student's experience of the task. He asked, 'Do you think you can manage that?' However, he pays insufficient attention to the student's reaction. There is insufficient *tuning or empathic communication*.

The student is not encouraged to consider this task an achievable challenge. There is no reason for him to have any feelings of confidence or competence. It is more likely he will feel the opposite. His negative feelings will increase. He will not see rewards for his efforts. This example illustrates the major role that inadequate instruction or explanation plays in the development and maintenance of a positive (or negative) attributional style.

Scenario 2

T:	This is your task. I have given you some cubes so that you can use them to help you to work out the first few examples.

S:	(Nods)

T:	You have to do these six rows of sums, but let's start with this one. Tell me, what does $14 \div 2$ mean again?

S:	That I have to divide 14 into two lots.

T:	Well done! You are well focused today. So take 14 cubes and divide them between two children. If you don't know the answers right away in your head, you can use the cubes and share them out on the table. Show me how to do $14 \div 2$ using the cubes.

S:	(Counts out 14 cubes)

T:	Do you think you can do the division now?

S:	Yes, you just have to take the cubes and divide them into two piles.

T:	Good, now try doing this first row of questions by using the cubes to help you. When I come back, I am sure you will have finished the first row. So, if you finish early you can start on the second row. I will be so pleased if you can complete the whole exercise by the end of the lesson.

The teacher leaves and the student begins working on the questions. When the teacher returns after five minutes the student is already working on the second row.

T: I see you have finished the first row without having to use the cubes every time. Well done!

S: It's not difficult now. When I don't know how to do a question I just use the cubes.

After 20 minutes the teacher returns.

T: You have done everything yourself! Excellent! Is that better than you thought you would do?

S: Yes. I thought I would only manage about three questions.

T: Why do you think you were able to do much better and do all the questions?

The student is actively involved in the instruction. Also, the student's reactions generate positive feelings about his professional skills in the teacher. The student appreciates the teacher's active involvement in the task he has to perform and experiences positive feelings and expectations regarding his own efforts mainly due to the teacher's use of positive comments and the experience of success. Although the teacher and the student may have different perspectives on the interchanges, those perspectives complement each other (as in Transactional Analysis).

Acknowledgement

These two scenarios were provided by Hans Harmsen and Rob van Elswijk.

CHAPTER 17

SUMMING UP

This book evolved from concerns about the classroom behaviours, motivation and attitudes of pupils with special needs. This led to an investigation into the classroom behaviours of pupils with special needs, and ways to address them at different levels of intervention. Intervention at the lower levels is more likely to address the problem temporarily, whereas the higher levels of intervention are more likely to lead to long-term benefits. However, intervention at the lower levels may well pre-empt the development of more serious and entrenched behaviours and may help to build long-term gains.

RECAP ON INTERVENTIONS
Classroom management techniques and personal organization issues

Classroom management techniques can fall into two categories:

1. Adjustments based on awareness and acknowledgement of the difficulty, for example:

    •   giving a direct reminder to start a task

    •   placing the pupil near the teacher where he can be refocused (discreetly).

2. A proactive intervention, for example:

    •   using modified worksheets

    •   planning the lesson structure

    •   using writing frames.

Social skills and communication issues

Examples of social competence training and communication skills include:

•   noticing 'triggers' and patterns of behaviour and addressing them with the student

- using Transactional Analysis and communication skills
- teaching the four stages, 'Stop – Analyse – Select – Act', via a social skills training programme or drama
- developing a positive attributional style and resilience.

Emotional support and guidance issues

Examples of emotional support and guidance include:

- improving and supporting self-esteem, self-concept and self-image, self-confidence
- developing a positive attributional style.

Pupils with SEND

Pupils with Special Educational Needs and Disability (SEND) need to be known well and understood or interventions will be inconsistent, ineffective and possibly inappropriate. There should be frequent 'Staffings' (a discussion about the student with as many of those involved, teachers and ancillary staff, as possible) to collate all the reactions and observations of all who work with that pupil. (The CBL may help as a focus for observations.) The information gathered must be shared with all who work with the pupil.

CONCLUSION

Any intervention, at whatever level, will need to acknowledge and be appropriate to the learning difficulties of the pupil. For example, it would be of little use starting a half-hour discourse on the application of cognitive behaviour therapy with a pupil with severe ADD. It would be challenging for a dyslexic pupil to handle a six-stage sequential coping strategy. An Asperger pupil may well find it difficult to translate a learnt social skill to a new situation without significant amounts of practise.

Many pupils with learning difficulties will need significant over-learning to internalize new social skills and to be able to generalize those skills into social competence. Even then this outcome may not happen without specific guidance and instruction.

It has been said that truly top rate fighter pilots have the skill to prioritize their reactions to a challenging situation and to constantly adjust and fine tune their reactions in response to the changing nature of the situation. You could say that a good teacher working with a challenging pupil has similar skills!

References

ADD Journeys (2009) *ADD Journeys with Sari Solden*. Available at http://addjourneys.com/members/sarisolden, accessed 10 July 2009.

Ahuja, A. (2009) 'Supermarket trolleys make us behave badly.' *The Times*, 22 January 2009, p.26.

ARROW (2009) *ARROW (Aural – Read – Respond – Oral –Write) website*. Available at www.self-voice.com, accessed 10 July 2009.

Barrow, G., Bradshaw, E. and Newton, T. (2001) *Improving Behaviour and Raising Self-Esteem in the Classroom*. London: David Fulton.

Bennett, T. (2009) *Class Act. A TES Essential Guide to Behaviour Management*. London: Times Edcational Supplement.

Berne, E. (1975) *What Do You Say After You Say Hello? The Psychology of Human Destiny*. London: Corgi.

Bloom, B.S. (1956) T*axonomy of Educational Objectives, Handbook I: The Cognitive Domain*. New York: David McKay.

British Association of Behavioural Optometrists (BABO) (2009) *British Association of Behavioural Optometrists website*. Available at www.babo.co.uk, accessed 10 July 2009.

Burden, R.L. (2005) *Dyslexia and Self-Concept*. London: Whurr.

Buzan, T. with Buzan, B. (2000) *The Mind Map Book*. Harlow: BBC Worldwide.

Chinn, S.J. (1996) 'The relationship between the grades received in GCSE mathematics by 26 students and their scores on the WISC.' *Dyslexia Review 7*, 8–9.

Circletime (2009) *Circletime and the Co-operative Classroom Resources website*. Available at www.circletime.co.uk, accessed 10 July 2009.

Crossbow Education (2009) *Crossbow Education: Learning Tools Anyone Can Grab*. Available at www.crossboweducation.com, accessed 10 July 2009.

Department for Education and Skills (DfES) (2001) *Special Educational Needs. Code of Practice*. November 2001. DfES/581/2001. London: DfES.

Department for Education and Skills (DfES) (2005) *Social and Emotional Aspects of Learning Guidance: Improving Behaviour, Improving Learning. Primary National Strategy DfES 1378*. London: DfES. Available at http://nationalstrategies.standards.dcsf.gov.uk/node/87009, accessed 10 July 2009.

Dunning, D., Heath, C. and Suls, J.M. (2004) 'Flawed self assessment.' *Psychological Science in the Public Interest 5*, 69–106.

Edwards, J.H. (1994) *The Scars of Dyslexia: Eight Case Studies in Emotional Reactions*. London: Cassell.

Gardner, H. (1999) *Intelligence Reframed: Multiple Intelligences for the 21st Century*. New York: Basic Books.

Harris, T.A. (1969) *I'm OK – You're OK*. London: Arrow.

Hattie, J. (2009) *Visible Learning: A Synthesis of Over 800 Meta-analyses Relating to Achievement*. Abingdon: Routledge.

Johnson, D., Johnson, R., Johnson Holubec, E. and Roy, P. (1984) *Circles of Learning*. Alexandria, VA: ASCD.

Keizer, K., Lindenberg, S. and Steg, L. (2008) 'The spreading of disorder.' *Science 322*, 85908, 1681–1685.

Krutetskii, V.A. (1976) *The Psychology of Mathematical Abilities in Schoolchildren*. Chicago: Chicago University Press.

Lawrence, D. (1996) *Enhancing Self-Esteem in the Classroom*. London: Paul Chapman.

McKay, N (2005) *Removing Dyslexia as a Barrier to Achievement: The Dyslexia Friendly Schools Toolkit*. Wakefield: SEN Marketing

McKinney, J.D.. (1990) 'Longitudinal Research on the Behavioural Characteristics of Children with Learning Difficulties.' In J.K. Torgesen (ed.) *Cognitive and Behavioural Characteristics of Children with Learning Disabilities*. Austin, TX: Pro-Ed.

Mortimore, T. (2003) *Dyslexia and Learning Style*. London: Whurr.

Myers, D.G. (1993) T*he Pursuit of Happiness*. New York: Harper Paperbacks.

National Deaf Children's Society (2009) 'Classrooms with good acoustics have been shown to improve pupil behaviour.' *Times Educational Supplement (TES)*, 30 January, 10.

Office for Standards in Education (Ofsted) (2001) *Improving Attendance and Behaviour in Secondary Schools.* London: Ofsted. Available at www.ofsted.gov.uk/Ofsted-home/Publications-and-research/Browse-all-by/Documents-by-type/Thematic-reports/Improving-attendance-and-behaviour-in-secondary-schools-2001, accessed 10 July 2009.

Reid Lyon, G., Shaywitz, S.E. and Shaywitz, B.A. (2003) 'A definition of dyslexia.' *Annals of Dyslexia 53*, 1–15.

Seligman, M.E.P. (2006) *Learned Optimism: How to Change Your Mind and Your Life.* New York: Vintage Books.

Spence, S.H. (1995) *Social Skills Training.* Slough: NFER-Nelson.

Thomson, M. and Chinn, S. (2001) 'Good Practice in Secondary School.' In A. Fawcett (ed.) *Dyslexia: Theory and Good Practice.* London: Whurr.

Torgesen, J.K. (ed.) (1990) *Cognitive and Behavioural Characteristics of Children with Learning Disabilities.* Austin, TX: Pro-Ed.

UPS of Downs (2009) *'The UPS of Downs: Down Syndrome Support for Families.'* Available at www.theupsofdowns.co.uk, accessed 10 July 2009.

Veenhoven, R. (2006) *World Database of Happiness, Happiness in Nations, Rank Report 2006-1.* Rotterdam: Erasmus University. Available at http://worlddatabaseofhappiness.eur.nl, accessed 7 October 2009.

Wainwright, G.R. (2003) *Teach Yourself Body Language.* London: Hodder Education.

Weiner, B. (1985) 'An attributional theory of achievement, motivation and emotion.' *Psychological Review 92*, 548–573.

Wilson, J., Williams, N. and Sugarman, B. (1967) *Introduction to Moral Education.* London: Pelican.

Yazbak, F.E. (2003) Autism in the United States: a Perspective. J*ournal of American Physicians and Surgeons. 8*, 4, 103–107.

Further Reading

Attwood, T. (1998) *Asperger Syndrome*. London: Jessica Kingsley Publishers.

Berne, E. (1964) *Games People Play*. London: Penguin.

Betts, D.E. and Patrick, N.J. (2008) *Hints and Tips for Helping Children with Autism Spectrum Disorders*. London: Jessica Kingsley Publishers.

Burden, R.L. (2000) *The Myself-as-a-Learner Scale (MALS)*. Slough: NFER-Nelson.

Cooper, P. and O'Regan, F.J. (2001) *Educating Children with AD/HD*. London: RoutledgeFalmer.

Corrie, L. (2002) *Investigating Troublesome Classroom Behaviour*. London: RoutledgeFalmer.

Crone, D.A., Horner, R.H. and Hawken, L.S. (2004) *Responding to Problem Behaviour in Schools*. New York: Guilford Press.

Csoti, M. (2001) *Social Awareness Skills for Children*. London: Jessica Kingsley Publishers.

Dweck, C.S. (2000) *Self Theories*. Hove, UK: Psychology Press.

Foster, J. (2004) *Target: Self-Esteem*. Edinburgh: Barrington Stoke.

Gray, P., Miller, A. and Noakes, J. (eds) (1995) *Challenging Behaviour in Schools*. London: Routledge.

Hamblin, D. (1993) *The Teacher and Counselling*. Hemel Hempstead: Simon & Schuster.

Janis-Norton, N. (2004) *In Step with Your Class*. Edinburgh: Barrington Stoke.

Krathwohl, D.R., Bloom, B.S. and Masia, B.B. (1973) *Taxonomy of Educational Objectives, the Classification of Educational Goals. Handbook II: Affective Domain*. New York: David McKay.

Lane, C. and Chinn, S. (1986) 'Learning by self-voice echo.' Academic Therapy 21, 4, 477–481.

Levine, M. (1990) *Keeping a Head in School*. Cambridge, MA: Educators Publishing Service.

Levine, M. (1993) *All Kinds of Minds*. Cambridge, MA: Educators Publishing Service.

Levine, M. (1994) *Educational Care*. Cambridge, MA: Educators Publishing Service.

Long, R. (2002) *Behaviour Matters: A Whole-Class Behaviour Audit*. Rob Long (tel. 01803 866 745) Available from www.behaviourmatters.com/publications.htm, accessed 8 July 2009.

Morris, D. (1982) *The Pocket Guide to Manwatching*. London: Triad Granada.

Moyes, R.A. (2002) A*ddressing the Challenging Behaviour of Children with High-Functioning Autism/Asperger Syndrome in the Classroom*. London: Jessica Kingsley Publishers.

Plummer, D. (2001) *Helping Children to Build Self-Esteem*. London: Jessica Kingsley Publishers.

Rogers, B. (2000) *Classroom Behaviour: A Practical Guide to Effective Teaching and Behaviour Management*. London: Sage.

Seach, D. (1998) *Autistic Spectrum Disorder*. Tamworth, UK: NASEN (National Association of Special Educational Needs).

Woliver, R. (2008) *Alphabet Kids: From ADD to Zellweger Syndrome*. London: Jessica Kingsley Publishers.

Resources and Useful Organizations

ADHD
www.livingwithadhd.co.uk

www.ADHD.org.uk

Aspergers Syndrome Foundation
www.aspergerfoundation.org.uk

Autism Education Trust
www.autismeducationtrust.org.uk

British Association of Behavioural Optometrists
www.babo.co.uk

The British Dyslexia Association
www.bdadyslexia.org.uk

The British government website for inclusion
http://inclusion.ngfl.gov.uk/index.php?i=240

Circle of Inclusion (A USA website aimed at early years providers and supporting inclusive practice)
http://www.circleofinclusion.org/

Down syndrome
www.theupsofdowns.co.uk

Dyslexia Action
www.dyslexiaaction.org.uk

Dyspraxia
www.dyspraxiafoundation.org.uk

iANSYST (software)
www.iansyst.co.uk

The International Dyslexia Association
www.interdys.org

Medical conditions at school
www.medicalconditionsatschool.org.uk

National Autistic Society
www.nas.org.uk

Prader-Willi Syndrome
www.pwsa.co.uk

Rob Long (behaviour management expert) site
www.roblong.co.uk

Royal National Institute for the Blind
www.rnib.org.uk

Speech, language and communication impairments
www.afasic.org.uk

Index

self-esteem 97–9
  defined 97–8
  impact of attributional style 117–19
Seligman, M.E.P. 116–21, 126
sensory stimulation, perceptual
    problems 24
Shaywitz, B.A. 21
Shaywitz, S.E. 21
short-sightedness 48
short-term memory 49–50
sleep problems 19
slow processing 51
social communication 90–1
  interventions 67
  and transactional analysis 102–15
social competence 89–90
  definitions 88
  key skills and requirements 88–93
  role of moral development 92–3
  subskills for effective communication
    90–1
social interactions
  problem behaviours 87
  providing support 68–9
  skills needed 88–93
social skills
  definitions 87
  forms and action sequences 88–92
  subskills affecting communication
    90–1, 102
  training programmes 66, 74–5,
    89–91
special needs in classrooms 15–27
  background and characteristics
    15–16
  common conditions 16–27
  comorbid conditions 27
  rare disorders 45–7
  recording classroom behaviours
    32–44
speech and language disorders 25–6
  key concerns 42
  recording classroom behaviours 41–2
speech-recognition software 76
spelling, and IQ 94
spelling problems 23
  marking and corrections 79
Spence, S.H. 90–1, 102
starting activities
  lack of confidence 67–8
  needing individual attention 58,
    61–2
  slowness problems 58, 60–1
  teacher interventions and solutions
    60–2, 67–8, 75
  using frameworks and structures 75
'strokes' (TA) 112, 113
stubbornness 47
stuttering 26
success
  and attributional style 117–18
  characteristics 120
  key requirements 124–6

Sugarman, B. 92–3
Suls, J.M. 119
swearing 47

TA see Transactional Analysis
task completion difficulties 58–9
  giving extra time 62–3, 71–2
  teacher interventions 63–4
teacher attitudes
  and pupil perceptions 78–9
  pupil performance expectations 80,
    98
  to dyslexia/ADD 81
teacher interventions and strategies
    60–9, 71–6, 134–5
  key actions 134–5
  developing positive attributional
    styles 56, 98–9, 116–32
  social skills training programmes 66,
    74–5, 89–91
  use of Transactional Analysis 101–15
teacher training, and rare disorders 46
teaching styles
  directive and responsive expressions
    114–15
  importance of consistency 69
  speed of delivery issues 80
'theory of multiple intelligences'
    (Gardner) 51, 94–6
tics and jerking movements 47
timekeeping problems 58
  allowing extra time 62–3, 71–2
Torgesen, J.K. 18
Tourette syndrome 19, 47
  incidence and prevalence 46
training see teacher training
Transactional Analysis 101–15
  ego states 103–7
  understanding individual transactions
    108–15

UPS of Downs 46

'vanilla environment' 63
Veenhoven, R. 124
Visible Learning: A Synthesis of Over 800
    Meta-analyses Relating to Achievement
    (Hattie 2009) 73–4, 87
vision problems 48
voice-input software 76

Wainwright, G.R. 104
Wechsler Intelligence Scale for Children
    (WISC) 94
Weiner, B. 117
Williams, N. 92–3
Wilson, J. 92–3
work initiation problems see starting
    activities
working memory 50
worksheets 62, 64

writing difficulties 22–3
  completion problems 58, 62–3
  giving extra time 62–3, 71–2

Yazbak, F.E. 19

371.904

Lightning Source UK Ltd.
Milton Keynes UK
UKOW011021141112

202191UK00003B/1/P

9 781849 050500